GETTING INTO RADIO-CONTROLLED SPORTS

GETTING INTO RADIO-CONTROLLED SPORTS

Jerry Murray

G. P. Putnam's Sons • New York

Library of Congress Cataloging in Publication Data

Murray, Jerry.
Getting into radio-controlled sports.
Includes index.
SUMMARY: Discusses radio-controlled devices used to
power models in the air and water and on land.
1.   Models and modelmaking—Radio control systems—
Juvenile literature.   [1.   Models and modelmaking—Radio
control systems]   I.   Title.
TT154.5.M87   629.04′022′8   78-31751
ISBN 0-399-20686-8

Contents

1

The Small World of R/C

There are three routes of adventure into the world of radio-controlled (R/C) modeling and sporting— through the air, through water, and on land. Along each of these routes there are byways and side trips that may lure the hobbyist into surprising new recreational territory. The truly ardent R/C hobbyist often travels up and down several of these routes simultaneously.

The usual R/C hobbyist chooses but one of the three escape routes, exploring it at an undemanding pace. The small world of R/C sporting can provide for the individual's total recreational needs or it may simply exist for a few years of constructively active fun.

R/C modeling is the constructive part of it all, and can be as large or as small as the hobbyist chooses. Preformed plastic kits can be had which snap together in a matter of minutes to make a car or boat or plane that can be put into use that very day. Other kits are made up of tiny sticks and delicate parts to be cut and fitted together according to detailed plans; these pieces may take weeks or months to emerge fully from the box as the miniature version of the hobbyist's most cherished vehicle. Or, from nothing more than a drawing found in a history book, the R/C modeling craftsman can recreate that romantic part of history and make it come to life.

R/C sporting is the active part in this extraordinary area of fun. It takes skill and coordination to send a race car speeding over a tortuously twisting track, to jibe and tack with a sleek sailing sloop, to make that racy red biplane loop and soar through the air. These sporting skills are closely coupled with the modelist's construction. R/C sporting skills take some learning, and that

Hobby show displays like this attract many people to the small world of R/C. Active R/C clubs attract even more.

learning comes more easily when it is helped by the intimate knowledge of just how a model craft was put together. The R/C sporter does not necessarily have to be an R/C modelist, but the construction of the model aids in the enjoyment of its use.

It's a vicarious sort of enjoyment, but it's not a fleeting craze. The small world of R/C is a highly refined version of a world that's been visited by mankind for centuries. Stone Age men and women used sharp stones and charcoal-tipped sticks to create miniature worlds on the walls of their caves, and they used the flickering light from campfires to make their drawings move and come to life. When an ancient sailing vessel embarked on a long and perilous voyage, some of those left behind built and sailed the ship in miniature; as they did this, their hopes and thoughts were with those daring men of the sea who had gone off to face the terrors and thrills of the unknown. Long before mankind took to the skies, inventors built miniature versions of flying ships and sent them aloft with the birds. Countless wars have been fought in small scale by generals who never heard the sound of cannon. Boys and girls throughout the world have lived the lives of grown-ups in a doll's house. Great works of fiction have been written about Liliputian life. But it is the miniature vehicle that has continued to capture human imagination through the ages. And miniaturized radio circuitry at long last lets anyone make small vehicles that actually work in a miniature world.

There are frustrations involved in the miniature world of R/C. The race car modelist forgets to charge a battery in his radio gear and becomes a spectator instead of a driver at the races. The ship modelist runs the craft aground and must slog through the water like a foolish giant to set it free. The R/C model pilot makes a false move and watches helplessly as the work of a winter goes into a tailspin from which it never recovers. Or radio waves from a passing police car may send the model out of the modelist's transmitter range until the little craft disappears from view. Small it might be, but the R/C world is a very real world, complete with its healthy share of frustrations and problems.

Of course the problems are part of the pleasures, for pleasures that come too easily do not endure. However, the world in miniature has endured, and now with a boost from miniature circuitry, it is spreading quickly. It seems as if almost everybody is getting into the R/C act. There are hundreds of R/C modelist supply manufacturers who ship their products to hobby shops all over the world. There are thousands of hobby shops, and this number is growing daily as R/C sporters form clubs that not only allow for many types of R/C competition, but also draw more people into the pastime.

Indeed it's more than a pastime. The R/C world is a recreational activity in the truest sense. It allows the student to escape from the chores of his or her books to fight for the pole position at the International Grand Prix. It lets the landlocked attorney leave judges and

The world of R/C used to be inhabited exclusively by males. Now women and girls are enjoying the sport and the modeling too.

clients behind and patrol the English Channel in a fast torpedo boat. It takes the garage mechanic up through the smog in a sleek, home-built monoplane to play tag with an eagle. It sends the mind on fantastic trips of fancy during long winter months of careful construction, then sends it off on a new sort of trip as the model comes to life with the blooming of spring. The R/C world gives lessons in such things as aerodynamics, hydrodynamics, electronics, and internal combustion engines. But its greatest function is in revitalizing the work-weary human being.

If everyone does get into the R/C act, there is room for all with no crowding. An entire R/C world can exist in just a tiny corner of our large and crowded one. A complete Indy track can lie dormant for six days of the week, disguised as a parking lot, then change into a noisy arena filled with cheering spectators and daringly competing race car drivers on Sunday. The backyard swimming pool can become the sleek gray submarine's waters. The city park quickly converts to a bustling aerodrome from which the *Spirit of St. Louis* takes off for Paris, ignoring the dog-fighting warplanes and the silently soaring gliders above.

R/C worlds exist all around us. It is surprisingly easy to get in and out of them once you know where they are. It is not, however, so easy to leave these R/C worlds forever, because once you have visited these vicarious worlds, their lure is strong.

2

The Guiding Hands

The guiding hands will be yours. Your hands will surely be quaking the first time you set out to put your model through its paces, but with help and practice you'll soon be astounded at the complex commands you can send out from the box in your hands to your very responsive model. That model soon will become an extension of yourself. Although radio controlling will always remain a challenge, those first unsure movements of control sticks and levers and wheels in time will become second nature to you.

Even on your first try at handling the transmitter, your guiding hands will control your craft with a great deal more ease than was ever conceived by the R/C pioneers. Today's sophisticated radio gear is so reliable that you may never have to look inside the transmitter box except to change batteries once a year. But within the box and within the model is hardware that every serious modeler should understand, plus a great deal of imaginative work by the pathfinders to the world of R/C.

Two brothers named William and Walter Goode and a man named Jim Walker were the R/C pioneers. They were hobbyists, not commercial inventors, working jointly and independently to put controllable life into the models they made. Their developmental work took place in the thirties, in and around Washington, D.C. Gasoline and electric motors were available for modelists then, but the only means of controlling powered models were directly attached to the little craft. A model boat or car would be sent off to make its own way or it could race around a pivot point at the end of a cable. A model airplane could be sent off in free flight or it could be moved up and down in the air at the end of a pair of U-control lines. The modelist had a choice of a runaway or a puppet, neither of which could be equipped with any sort of device to control its speed.

Radio gear was available then, too, but it was extremely heavy and cumbersome. It was all right for making the big Philco console radio talk, but far too heavy and fragile to be sent aloft in a miniature airplane or across a windswept pond in a little boat. But Walker and the Goode brothers were severely infected with the germs of modeler's disease, a malady that makes the infected person view every bit of hardware in sight as something that might become part of a model. These pioneer modelists disassembled their parlor radios, their automobiles, and their telephones in order to make an R/C model. And since their infection was deep, they chose the most challenging model to work with, the airplane.

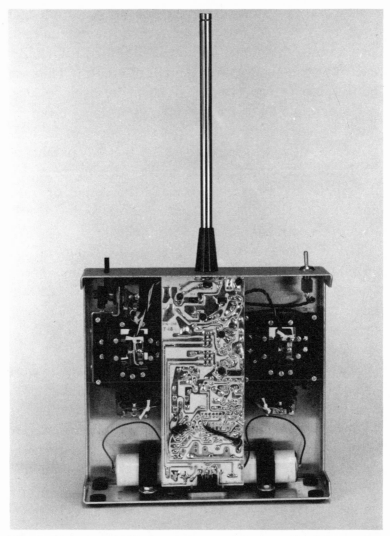

The inside of an R/C transmitter, with control stick mechanisms at each side, printed circuit board in the center, and rechargable Cd-Ni batteries below. (Courtesy Kraft Systems, Inc.)

The first R/C transmitter was too heavy for one man to carry. Two car batteries were used to send the radio signal up to the model airplane. The radio transmitter had only one signal, one channel of control. This was quite a step up from none at all. Up in the airplane, glass vacuum tubes taken from a radio console received the radio signal and passed it on to a system of battery-powered relays which jerked a lever this way or that and made the airplane's rudder move. It took over five pounds of that early gear to make the rudder operate, and it took a model airplane with a seven-foot wingspan to get this agonizing payload off the ground.

The R/C pioneers didn't always get things off the ground. Even today's model airplane engines aren't always easy to start, and there were days when the R/C pioneers headed back to the hangar with nothing more than a few backfires to show for their efforts as inventors.

Countless hours of creative thought and labor were invested toward the doubtful reward of making a toy airplane lift itself off the ground and fly around in a few wavering circles before making some kind of haphazard landing. Once the balky engine got the cumbersome craft in the air, a digit was dialed on the telephone part of the circuitry, and the airplane responded with a violent turn and with the loss of altitude that goes with such a crude maneuver.

Another quickly dialed digit would yank the rudder back to its neutral position, so the whirling propeller might gain some precious altitude for the craft. Still another dialed digit would sock the rudder over in the opposite direction. The plane wouldn't land till it ran out of gas. Subtle maneuvers were out of the question with this crude radio gear, but it worked. The puppet's strings had been cut, and now there was a way to reach out and turn the runaway model around.

World War II came along, and with it many advances in science and industry. Among the developments begun in those years were penicillin, the jet engine, and improved underwater diving gear for the fishermen of the world. All these things of course didn't help R/C modelers at all. However, the R/C pioneers helped the war effort by installing their ungainly gear in aircraft gunners' target drones, and by making the drones dodge bullets in a miniature war of their own.

Not until after the war did three scientific developments drastically change R/C and a great many other electronics inventions, such as television and electronic calculators. These developments were the tiny wafers of silicon transistors which replaced the world's vacuum tubes, the printed circuit boards which did away with masses of tangled wires, and the cadmium-nickel (Cd-Ni) battery which was so much more efficient than the carbon dry cell.

The developments came in rapid succession, and as each emerged from the industrial laboratory, modelers placed it in their crafts. Everywhere in the industrial world—on land, on water, and in the air—crude R/C models with strange assortments of components and circuitry were moving about on their own. It had taken centuries, but at last the miniaturist had tiny controls for his models.

For a while businessmen were absorbed with much vaster projects, and modelers were too busy scrounging for weird new parts to build the R/C model they'd see in an article appearing in *Popular Mechanics* or a similar publication. But some of those R/C modelers and sporters found time to start companies that today turn out very reliable R/C radio gear. Phil Kraft was one of these businessmen/modelers, and Paul Runge was another. Kraft started out in his garage, and now has 250 employees producing radio gear for modelists at Kraft Systems, Inc. in Vista, California. Runge had a similar start with his Ace R/C, Inc., in Higginsville, Missouri. Each had problems in getting his business off the ground, for bankers are not noted for lending money to toy makers who operate out of a family garage. And no one could foresee the coming boom in recreational enterprises.

Relics of the early days of R/C modeling are rare. The early radio controlling gear found its way back into the family car and the parlor radio, and the early models rarely survived more than a few flights. The Smithsonian Institution's National Air and Space Museum has a few of these relics on display. One is the model airplane called *Guff,* which is considered to be the first practical R/C model, and dates back to 1937. Another old-timer is called the *Liberty Bell,* a single-channel R/C airplane, powered by a carbon dioxide motor, which was flown across the United States by pilots who followed its flight from below.

Today more than a dozen companies manufacture radio gear in Japan and the United States. Variations in the gear are slight, but at times significant. With the exception of the little used pulse proportional R/C gear, all other modelist radio equipment is of the digital proportional type. This provides much more than the all-or-nothing sort of control enjoyed by the R/C pioneers. It allows for subtle changes in control. Digital proportional means that for every movement of a control stick or lever on the radio transmitter, there is a proportional movement of the device in the model which controls its direction or speed or some piece of auxiliary equipment. The hand that moves on the transmitter simultaneously moves on the model.

The simplest of the digital proportional systems is the two-channel, two-stick radio. One control stick on the transmitter moves to the left and right, the other moves forward and back. The movement of either stick sends an electrical signal to the radio crystal, which forwards it on to the receiver in the model by means of the power in the transmitter batteries. The greater the movement of the control stick, the greater the signal is when it goes through the extended aerial on the transmitter and on to the antenna in the model. The receiver in the model sends an electrical signal on to a servomechanism, which is powered by the battery pack in the model and which performs the control work indicated by the control stick on the transmitter.

The servo consists of a miniaturized radio signal amplifier and a tiny electrical motor, both contained in a plastic box. The motor runs in either direction and operates a lever or a wheel connected through the plastic case to the tiny motor's shaft. The two-channel radio operates two different servos, and the servos can be operated either one at a time or together. With the proper linkage, a servo can operate a rudder or a steering suspension, airplane elevators or ailerons, a throttle, or a sail, or a switch on another motor in the model.

The two-channel airplane is usually a glider. The stick that moves to the left and right operates the rudder servo, and the forward and back stick works the plane's elevators. Pushing the stick forward makes the elevators and the airplane go down, and pulling it back does the reverse. When either stick is released, it springs back to the neutral position. Each control stick should have a trim lever with it. Models don't always move straight and true when their controls are at neutral. The trim levers allow for making small adjustments in the electronic controls so that the modelist does not have to continually jockey about with a control stick to keep the model on an even course.

The two-stick, two-channel radio is fine for operating racing cars and boats. One channel controls speed, the other direction. A refinement that many American R/C

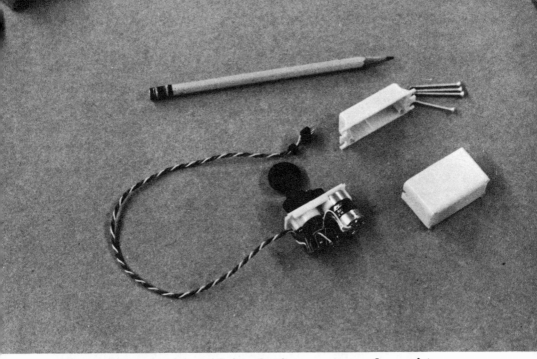

The servo mechanism with its plastic case removed, consisting of a micro-circuited amplifier and a miniaturized DC electric motor. (Courtesy Kraft Systems, Inc.)

car racers use is the transmitter made with a miniature steering wheel in place of a steering stick. The Futaba radio gear features this, and that manufacturer claims to have extremely rugged servos which will stand up to the heavy vibration encountered with R/C racing cars. Futaba's transmitter for race cars has a lever type throttle control on its side instead of the standard second control stick on the front of the box. Futaba specializes for the R/C race car driver, and JoMac and Kraft are now following suit. Some American R/C race car drivers add their own refinement by replacing the throttle lever with a spring-loaded, pistol-grip throttle of the type used by slot car racers. Radio manufacturers specialize, but most of them still specialize toward the R/C airplane.

The one-stick, two-channel transmitter is favored by R/C glider enthusiasts. The single stick gimbals in any direction, making it easier to direct the simple stunt maneuvers that gliders can perform. Releasing the spring-loaded stick returns the rudder and elevators to their neutral positions and straightens the glider out into level flight. This comes in very handy when the common problem of overcontrolling has placed the glider in an uncomfortable position high in the sky.

Additional channels provide for more controls and for more auxiliary equipment on the model. Additional controls are particularly needed for flying the powered R/C airplane. Auxiliary equipment is particularly favored by the scale model boat builder who wants to add realistic functions to the craft.

The three-channel radio opens more doors for the modelist. The third channel could be used for controlling ailerons on an aerobatic glider. Or it could be used to control a throttle on a power plane, although in this case the control would not be spring-loaded, since flying an airplane does not call for the constant speed changes involved with a racing car or a speedboat. The third channel on a sailboat's transmitter could be used to control a jib sail, with the first two channels being used to control the mainsail and the rudder.

As the modelist gets deeper into R/C, more functions are desired to make the models function better and more realistically. The fourth channel on a powered airplane model could go for ailerons, the fifth might go for carburetor mixture control, and a sixth could be used for retracting landing gear. As one might suspect, more channels cost more money. At this time, Ace/RC is the only radio manufacturer that makes a radio to which additional channels can be added. R/C radios in kit form are available from electronics suppliers such as Heathkit, for those who enjoy the work and the savings of do-it-yourself electronic assembly. There is nothing magic about the R/C gear, and the experienced electronics hobbyist can build the radio and servos from scratch and come up with even more than the seven channels that manufacturers offer as the top of their line in equipment.

Auxiliary functions are the model shipbuilder's delight. However, the ship modeler, who normally has little concern about excess weight, may choose to save some money by using one channel to operate several devices on the model ship. This can be done by using the heavy relays that were the servos of the R/C pioneers. A relay is nothing more than an electrically operated switch. For instance, a small current sent to the relay opens or closes a circuit, allowing a large current to flow from a battery to a motor. Several relays can be operated by one servomechanism. One way to do this is to run a small current to a contact on the servo's moveable lever arm. Contacts leading to several relays can be arranged in the shape of an arc through which the lever arm swings on command. Then, with the control stick on the transmitter, the modelist can swing the servo's arm and pick out the relay to be activated by the batteries that operate the model ship.

The batteries in both the transmitter and the model have to be fully charged for decent operation. Most radio gear comes with a built-in battery charger. Follow the directions for your particular radio gear but, in general, recharge the batteries overnight on the night before you plan to do some R/C sporting. Plan on no more than one hour of sporting before the batteries will be so weak that your model may not respond to the controls.

Radio-control gear is no longer prohibitively expensive. There is a very adequate two-stick, two-channel Sanwa radio which is new to the market and sells for about eighty dollars. You may be able to get it for less through a hobby supply discount house, but it is better to pay the full price through your local hobby store. Hobby stores are the greatest promoters of R/C sports and are largely responsible for broadcasting the news about R/C club meetings, which attract more hobbyists into the field. The good hobby shop proprietor can also give you most helpful advice as you're getting into R/C. He wants to be helpful, for he must attract customers in order to make a decent profit and stay in business.

The price of radio gear has come down because of technical advances, but more importantly because of the greatly increasing numbers of people in the sport. This allows for less expensive mass production methods to be used by the manufacturers. As costs come down, there seems to be no limit to where R/C sports can go. However, the federal government has placed one irritating but very necessary limit on R/C sporting.

Our airwaves are crowded with television and radio signals—AM and FM—and with the transmissions of radio signals from CBers, police cars, the military, and others. Each of these signals can interfere with an R/C signal sent on the same radio frequency and can, indeed, completely overwhelm and blot out an R/C signal through the sheer weight of electrical wattage. The Federal Communications Commission determines who can use which frequencies and how much power can be used on those frequencies. Officials of the FCC, realizing the value of recreation, have assigned a number of frequencies for R/C modelists' use. The number is limited, as is the power which the R/Cer may legally use. One watt of power is all that is ever needed to operate the most multifunctional radio gear, and this is the FCC limit. But it has also limited the total number of R/C frequencies to seventeen. With some of these seventeen requiring a special license, the total number of R/C frequencies is not enough to operate more than about eight different models in any one place at any one time.

The radio crystal in the R/C transmitter determines the frequency. Some transmitters are built so that the crystal can be changed very easily. Each of the frequencies has a color code and an antenna flag which goes with it, so the modelist can tell at a glance if some other modelist is already using a certain frequency. If your frequency is being used, you can either change crystals or wait for the other modelist to finish his run or flight and turn off the switches on his transmitter and receiver. R/Cers are usually pretty good about this and won't hog a particular frequency for an unreasonable length of time. Various systems are set up at an R/C sporting site to help inform the modelist as to which frequencies are in use and to limit R/C sporting time on a crowded day.

FREQUENCIES AND FLAG COLORS

Megaherz (MHz)	Color
26.995	Brown
27.045	Red
27.095	Orange
27.145	Yellow
27.195	Green
53.1	Black and brown
53.2	Black and red
53.3	Black and orange
53.4	Black and yellow
53.5	Black and green
72.080*	White and brown
72.160	White and blue
72.240*	White and red
72.320	White and violet
72.400*	White and orange
72.960	White and yellow
75.640*	White and green

*Special license needed

The three groups of frequencies listed above may be referred to as the 11-meter, 6-meter and 4-meter bands, respectively. Each of the frequency groups has its own limitations and idiosyncracies. The 27 MHz frequency band is subject to interference from CBers who illegally operate on that channel, often with a whole lot of power. Everything in the 50 to 54 MHz frequency band was given by the FCC to ham radio operators a long time ago, and certain frequencies within this range were later assigned to R/Cers, but those R/Cers who operate in this frequency band are somehow still required to have a difficult to obtain ham radio operator's license in addition to their R/C license. And those radio frequencies in the 4-meter band which have been marked with an asterisk can only be used by R/Cers to operate model airplanes, not cars or boats.

The situation is a little confusing because the airways are crowded, and because commercial use of the airways takes precedence over use by hobbyists. Certain frequencies can't be used in certain areas because of powerful interference from radio systems that were put into use before the advent of R/C modeling. Around the Sacramento, California area, for instance, state police use much of the 72 MHz band, so a call from police headquarters can have a disastrous effect on an R/C model using that band. Private and commercial airplane pilots from Harris, Texas, use the 72.160 band for their communications and those from nearby Galveston use the 75.640 band. Since these pilots use radios with up to thirty watts of power, those two frequency bands can't be used by modelers in that particular area. The one-watt R/C transmitter isn't powerful enough to do much interfering with other radios in any area.

R/C transmitters do not have much power. It does not take much outside interference to disrupt a modeler's radio signal. By far the most common source of interference is the "glitch." No one knows the true source of the glitch. It may come from a radio-dispatched taxicab somewhere in the vicinity or from an airliner flying above the clouds. The troublesome glitch is simply a stray radio signal, coming from an unknown source, that temporarily interferes with the model's radio control. The perfectly made, perfectly controlled model can be sent astray by the glitch, usually at a very inopportune time. Beware of the glitch. But if your R/C model encounters the glitch with any sort of regularity, have your radio equipment checked out.

Your hobby shop proprietor can check your radio gear and tell you if it is the source of the glitches that have been troubling you. Also, there are multimeters especially made for R/C modelers to check out their own equipment. The most common source of the glitch is the run-down battery. The batteries in both the transmitter and in the model should be fully charged before you go out to do any R/C sporting. Even a freshly recharged battery can be the source of a glitch if the battery is old or defective. While Cd-Ni batteries last a long time and can be recharged many times, they do not last forever. By the time you get into a first-class

R/C model, you will probably want to have an R/C equipment meter such as the Power Pacer, made by L. R. Taylor & Co., or the Digipace, made by Ace R/C.

All R/Cers are required to get a license from the FCC to use their radio. The license costs no more than a postage stamp, and the application is available at your hobby shop. There's no test involved with getting the license, and the reason for licensing at all is so the FCC has an idea of how many R/Cers are active.

You may obtain your radio gear secondhand, but if you get into R/C in this fashion, be sure the gear works before you buy it. And be aware that secondhand gear does not come with a factory warranty. Have the seller show you, through demonstration, that all the channels function, that the servos and batteries function, and that the transmitter has enough range. This is best done by operating the model with which the seller used the radio gear. If that model isn't available, a general rule is that the transmitter should operate the servos at a distance of greater than thirty feet when the transmitter's antenna has been removed.

There is some argument about certain brands of radio gear being best for certain kinds of R/Cing. Some servos and receivers are undoubtedly a little more rugged than others and therefore should survive the heavy vibrations found in R/C race cars. Servos come in different sizes—small, medium, large, and the new miniature servos. There are too many different kinds of radio equipment to cover them completely here, and their differences are not very great. In general, don't buy radio gear with small servos if you're planning on building a big model. Check with active R/C modelists in the area of the sport you want to enter, and they can tell you what kind of radio gear is currently favored.

Whether you buy new or used radio gear, its repairs should, of course, be a factor in deciding what brand to purchase in the future. All radio gear is quite reliable now, but all of it can break down under rough conditions. All of it can be repaired, but some can be repaired more quickly and easily than others. It is maddening to have a model all built and ready to go, then find its transmitter isn't acting right.

Some cities have repair shops for R/C equipment, but most broken gear is sent back to the factory for repairs. Before you buy any radio, check with your **hobby shop proprietor.** More important, check with other modelists to see what kind of reliability and service record goes along with that brand of gear.

Kraft Systems boasts of having the quickest turnaround time for repairs, because of the great number of modelists among their employees who understand the frustrations of R/Cing without a radio. Kraft also boasts of having the best, longest warranty and of leading the field in developments. The firm has, for example, a preprogrammed transmitter, which by pressing a button, will send an airplane into the complex maneuver that's been programmed into the transmitter. Kraft reliability and good service comes at higher prices, in some instances, than those of some other companies. Listen to the advice of modeling friends before you buy your radio. If you're one of those rare modelers who can find no one to advise you, strongly consider buying the equipment made by the manufacturer whose plant is closest to you. You can find out manufacturers' addresses, and a great deal more, by investing two or three dollars in an R/C publication like *Model Builder* or *R/C Modeler*.

R/C Modeler is a publication meant for the more experienced modelist, and the magazine's editors are the first to admit this. The ads and the pictures are great for the beginner, but the text will largely be over the beginner's head. The magazine also publishes a nice little booklet titled *Radio Control . . . From the Ground Up* by Don Dewey. It is a very generalized booklet, and in it Dewey says, "If you were to pick up a copy of our publication, *R/C Modeler*, your first reaction would be one of complete confusion concerning the terminology used and the seeming intricacies and complexities of the sport. The same holds true for any sport or hobby whether it be bowling, golf, photography, archery, or guns and shooting. It is very much like the first day on a job or in school—the amount you seemingly have to learn appears to be overwhelming! But as each day progresses, the job becomes simpler and the jargon more understandable. The same holds true in any sport or hobby—you have to take the first step, and each succeeding step becomes easier and easier, until the original complexities become part of your own experience and storehouse of knowledge."

That is excellent advice, and the publication is a very

good one. Its editors offer a free sample copy of the magazine if you write to them at *R/C Modeler* Corporation, P.O. Box 487, Sierra Madre, California 91024. The magazine is largely oriented toward flying models, but covers cars and boats as well.

You may switch from one facet of R/C sporting to another, and you'll probably have more than one model. But your radio gear will be with you for some time, so be careful in its selection.

3

The Driving Force

Batteries are needed to operate your radio and servo gear, but an additional driving force is needed to make your model go. Most R/C modelists select one of three kinds of driving forces to get into the action part of the sport.

The wind is the simplest and cleanest of these. It's by far the cheapest, but it's also far from being the most reliable. The wind is an extremely powerful driving force, and it is a unique pleasure to harness a tiny portion of that force and put it to work in flying a model glider or sailing a model boat.

Remember that the wind can be capricious. An unexpected gust can capsize some sailboats or toss the glider or the powered plane into unexpected maneuvers. Or, just as suddenly, the wind can stop, the air can become very calm, leaving the sailboat helplessly adrift on the water or starting the glider on a stately descent toward earth. There are tricks and skills involved in harnessing the wind, in using it to your best advantage to win a sailboat race. Soaring birds know the tricks of finding and riding the invisible currents of air that can keep them aloft for hours, with no more than the smallest movements of the control surfaces of their wings and tails. The modelist's tricks and skills with the wind must be acquired, and are different for boats and planes. We will discuss those skills in later chapters, but for now bear in mind that wind power is the least expensive and the cleanest source of power available for model boat and plane enthusiasts.

The electric motor is ideal for operating some R/C boats and cars, and is just now becoming a practical driving force for R/C airplanes. The electric motor is small, clean, and reliable. It starts with the flick of a switch and can be closely controlled with a turn of a rheostat knob. Its direction can be reversed, which makes it still better for boats. By itself, the electric motor is the ideal driving force for almost any machine, except that this kind of motor needs an external source of energy. In the case of the R/C model, the energy comes from heavy, and often cumbersome, batteries.

For the ship modelist, the weight of the battery power source is usually used to advantage. Model ships and boats are the only kind of R/C crafts where weight is of little consideration. Some keenly competitive racing sailboats are ballasted with lead keels to weights of forty pounds. Almost all model ships need additional weight, properly placed, to keep them hull down in the water, and, consequently, often weigh more than forty pounds. The sailboats, of course, need no source of man-made driving power, and so their leaden weights are built into their keels. With a show-type boat, however, the lead ballast can be in the form of the heavy and cumbersome battery, which not only keeps the vessel hull down in the water, but also provides it with more than enough power to navigate for hours without returning to shore to have its batteries recharged.

The hulls of some model boats are large enough and buoyant enough to need the full weight of an automobile battery, precisely placed and well secured, to keep the hull balanced and realistically low in the water. A four-foot-long, one-foot-wide hull of a model freighter would be typical of the hull of one of these larger vessels. More typical in terms of size are the two-foot-long model ships and boats. These have a hull displacement that is very well suited for using a motorcycle battery for both ballast and power. As the size of the model gets smaller, so must the size of the battery.

Ordinary dry cell flashlight batteries are adequate for powering a small boat model. These last for only a very short time, however, before all their energy is discharged through the boat's propeller. This type of battery has the further disadvantage of a limiting voltage of one-and-one-half volts. The cadmium-nickel (Cd-Ni) dry cell is the battery of choice for the small boat R/C modeler and for electrically driven R/C cars and planes.

As might be expected, the Cd-Ni battery has a greater first cost than the carbon cell flashlight battery. Its rechargability more than makes up for its first cost and for the plug-in charger needed to restore its lost energy dozens and dozens of times. Several different voltages are available with Cd-Ni batteries, allowing for their use with more powerful motors. The most popular voltage among modelers is the six-volt variety. Banks of six-volt batteries can be wired up in series to provide power for twelve-volt motors, which are quite powerful. R/C modelists invariably prefer the rechargeable battery, whether it's the dry cell Cd-Ni type, or the wet cell lead sulfate automotive type battery.

Batteries are a necessary expense for the R/C modelist, as are electric motors, but the motor in your model boat does not have to be a costly one. The automotive junkyard can be an excellent source for the motor that powers your boat and for those that drive its auxiliary equipment. The motors that turn the screws on many a prize-winning model boat came from the doors of wrecked cars, where they were formerly used to roll the car's windows up and down. An elegant little model fire-fighting boat, which cruises the local model yacht basin and squirts a minispectacular jet of water from its fire gun, contains the workings of an automobile windshield washer pump and motor within its hull.

If you get into model boats, modeler's disease may drive you to some very unlikely places in search of the motor that fits in your model and does its job well. You'll run across an amazing variety of small electrical motors, quietly doing their jobs in surprisingly different places. While almost any electric motor can be geared

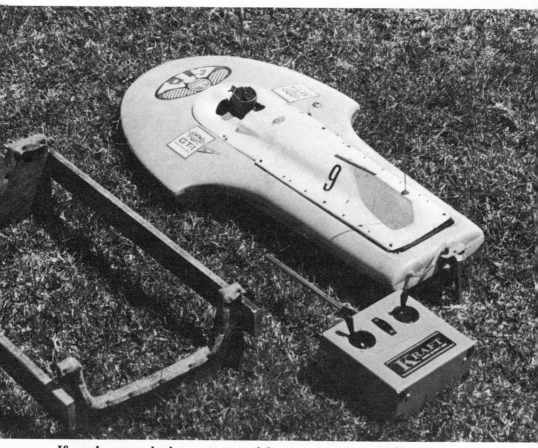

If you're very lucky, you can pick up an outdated R/C hydroplane, like this one found at a garage sale, complete with radio and motor, for twenty-five dollars.

or pulleyed to alter its speed, each does have a limit as to how much energy it can turn into power.

Few small electric motors bear nameplates that tell their power rating, so experimentation is often necessary to determine if the motor is just right for your needs. Logic can reduce the need for much of your experimentation. No matter how much gearing is used on the motor that turns the hands of a clock, for instance, that motor won't be capable of delivering enough power to the screw of a racing model speedboat or car.

The rheostat that serves as the throttling device for an electric motor is nothing more than a variable electrical resistance. The battery is a constant source of power. By writing a rheostat in between the battery and the motor, that constant power source may be changed by twisting the knob on the rheostat, either by hand or through remote control. All DC electric motors are reversible, and all battery-driven electric motors are DC.

Direct current wiring is quite simple and straightforward, with no shocking voltages involved. If you start out with an electrically operated model that you've bought in the form of a kit, the wiring instructions will be simply and clearly stated for you. If you continue with electrically driven R/C models, and as you advance to a point where you are designing and building models of your own, you'll need some help with the wiring. By then you'll need some auxiliary equipment such as a soldering gun and some electrical meters.

Boating club members will be only too happy to help you along with their knowledge and usually with their electrical tools. They know that you'll pass on the help they've given you when another novice joins the club.

In general, a balance is needed between voltage, current, and resistance. Since resistance increases with every faulty wiring connection, it is wise to insure the quality of those connections by learning proper soldering techniques and applying them.

The junkyard electrical motor won't do for some kinds of R/C models. Speedboats and racing cars and electric airplanes call for the small, specialized, high-speed motor expressly built for R/C modeling. In R/C sporting competition, these motors must comply with certain specifications to keep the racing model mechanically equal to others in its class. These small, high-speed motors handle a lot of power and generate considerable heat.

If you enter into class competition with an electric speedboat, the directions in your kit will ensure that construction will provide for the cooling air needed to keep the motor from burning itself out. If you design and build your own boat, be sure to give some consideration to air circulation for its motor. The high-speed electrical motor is often completely buried in the deepest recess of a boat model's hull, with one end of its shaft turning the screw that propels the boat and the other end turning a tiny propeller or fan which sucks cooling air in from above and circulates that air over the motor. The motor in the electrically driven car almost always has enough naturally circulating cooling air, and plans for electrically driven airplanes include this consideration.

Large, slow ships of full size employ massive screws which turn at very low speeds. The screw on a supertanker, for instance, turns at only 80 rpm, while the screw on a high-powered speedboat, on the other hand, may turn up to 10,000 rpm. Obviously, these two types of vessels use vastly different screws, and the difference is in more than merely the size. The screws on the big workboats are very deeply pitched, so that each of their slow revolutions takes a deep bite of water as the screw pushes the ship through the seas. The fast-turning screw of the speedboat, in contrast, has a much flatter pitch to it, although each of its flatter blades takes a big bite of water as the speedboat covers distance much more quickly than the plodding workboat. A wide variety of screws are available at your hobby shop, each one a reproduction of the screws that propel full-sized boats and ships.

Screws push a boat through the water and propellers pull a plane through the air. The propellers on some of the most fascinating R/C airplanes are electrically driven, and we will get into this type of airplane in a later chapter. At this time, the fuel-powered engine drives the vast majority of powered R/C airplanes, the bulk of the most competitive racing cars, and most competition speedboats. Most of these engines are variations of the same basic theme of the two-cycle, glow-plug engine, powered by fuel.

Most modelers use the terms gas and fuel inter-changeably. Strictly speaking, models all run on fuel. The fuel consists of a mixture of methyl alcohol (methanol), nitromethane, and a lubricant such as castor oil. The methanol promotes a smooth, relatively cool-burning operation, which is needed in conjunction with the hot-burning, high-powered nitromethane. The oil provides the lubrication for the engine, since the two-stroke engine has no crankcase or oil pump to circulate lubricant and keep the engine's parts running smoothly. Some modelers mix up their own fuel, saving themselves money and getting a mixture they feel is more powerful or which may have better lubrication properties. Premixed fuel is fairly expensive, but it is very convenient, and buying premixed fuel does away with the fire hazards involved with measuring and mixing volatile substances.

The basic small fuel-powered engine is very simple. Fuel from a tank that is built into the motor is gravity fed through an adjustable needle valve to the engine's crankcase, where it is vaporized by the engine's heat. The moving piston forces a mixture of fuel and air up through a port and into the engine's combustion chamber, where the piston compresses the mixture and the glow plug ignites it, forcing the piston down and turning the engine's crankshaft.

These little engines are miniature versions of many motorcycle engines, except that they have no car-buretors, piston rings, electrical ignition system or mufflers, and they have bronze bushings in place of ball bearings. The lack of a carburetor means that the small model engine can run at only one speed—wide open. The lack of rings and ball bearings means that it won't last as long as a full-sized engine or run as efficiently.

This is a minor consideration, however, since the small fuel engine runs efficiently enough, and since accidental disaster usually turns these inexpensive engines into junk before they can wear themselves out. The lack of a muffler means that they're noisy little devils, and while this provides still one more sense of vicarious enjoyment for some modelers, it has also created some local laws that have driven modelists out of city parks. The lack of an ignition system is a real joy.

The glow plug takes the place of a distributor, points and condenser, and a lot of intricate wiring. The glow plug is shaped like a spark plug, although it has no spark, and it screws into the cylinder head in the same fashion as a spark plug. Its fire comes from a tiny coil or bar of electrically resistant metal built into the end that fits inside the engine's combustion chamber. Hooking up one or two 1½-volt dry cell batteries to the glow plug's external end causes its internal coil to glow at red heat, which is enough to ignite the fuel and air mixture when the engine is cranked over by hand to the point where the mixture is compressed to its ignition pressure. A few drops of priming fuel is usually eyedroppered into the engine's exhaust ports to help get the thing going. Fuel combustion keeps the tip of the glow plug at red heat, and this red head continues to ignite the compressed fuel mixture after the battery has been

A .60 cu. in. fuel engine, sliced up to show its glow plug, the piston and its single ring, and the crankshaft which runs in ball bearings.

disconnected. The needle valve is then adjusted to maximum engine performance. These little engines turn up to 12,000 rpm, and while it can be a song to the ears of the modelist, it can be an irritant to the ears of the Sunday gardener. Various devices are available as carburetors, or throttling mechanisms, but most of these little engines run at all-out top speed till they run out of fuel.

Model engines are classified by their displacement, just as are full-sized engines. The smallest model engine has a displacement of .010 cubic inches, and the larger single cylinder engines go on up to a displacement of over one cubic inch. The smaller engines, running at top speed all the time, are not at all practical for R/C boats and cars, but they're fine for certain kinds of R/C airplanes. These airplanes are the auxiliary powered glider, an excellent airplane for the beginning pilot, and a few powered trainers and stunt planes with rather limited capabilities.

As fuel engines increase to about .1 cubic inch, there's room for a carburetor to throttle the speed of the engine and make a racing model truly competitive, or to vary the speed and the power of the serious stunting airplane. The Perry carburetor is the most widely accepted now, coming complete with high-speed and low-speed needle valves, an idling adjustment screw, and the butterfly-type valve, which meters in the fuel mixture to alter engine speed.

Engines of this size are big enough to accommodate some ball bearings on the crankshaft and some rings on the pistons. These larger engines may be fitted with mufflers, partially to quiet their high-speed noise, but also to improve on engine performance. The "tuned muffler" in use on cars, boats, and planes serves double duty by keeping the engine quiet and by bouncing some of the exhaust gas pressures back toward the engine's exhaust ports, quite effectively raising engine compression and, therefore, engine power.

All fuel engines, large or small, need a period of breaking in. This is frequently done on the modelist's workbench, with extra lubricating oil added to the fuel mixture, and cotton plugs added to the modelist's ears.

Smaller engines more often get their breaking-in period during use, with the modelist adjusting the needle valve so the engine is "running rich." The engine is definitely not running at peak performance then, but it is getting an extra dose of lubricating oil on its first few runs. Even after a breaking-in period on the workbench, where internal metal surfaces can work together in smoothing out tiny burrs and flaws while the engine runs under no load, it is still a good idea to run the engine rich for its first few times in sporting action.

Running rich or lean, in a boat or a car or a plane, something is sure to go wrong with your engine eventually. By working with the proper small tools, by working with care and thought, you can take your engine apart for an overhaul. The first time you do it is the tough time, the second time around is much easier, and you'll soon reach a point where you can tear down your Fox .30 and put it together again while you sit on the edge of the flying field and watch the flights of your friends.

Such engines as the Fox .30 need an occasional teardown, not because there's anything wrong with the engine design or construction, but because the Fox .30 is a favorite with R/C fliers, and sooner or later all R/C fliers crash their planes, and they always crash them nose-first. This unfortunate state of affairs bends crankshafts, which then need to be replaced. Even more often, a crash gets a bit of dirt in the engine's air intake, and only a very small bit of dirt is needed to ruin an engine of this size. After any crash where the engine digs dirt, the careful modelist takes the engine out of the airplane, tears it down and inspects it and cleans it and oils it.

R/C car engines are subject to ingesting dirt, too, not so much from their crashes, but from the dust that's raised by the six or eight other cars screaming around the track with them. R/C dune buggies, which are hugely popular in Japan, are particularly susceptible to engine damage from the dust that's raised from the dirt race courses. All fuel-powered R/C cars must have an adequate air filter on their carburetors, and those little air filters must be changed or cleaned when dust plugs them up to a point where the engine is gasping for air.

R/C fuel-powered engines used in boats don't need any air filters. But those engines need to be torn down and dried out and lubricated after a race course disaster sends the boat somersaulting over the water to rest with its keel in the air and its engine softly sizzling in the water.

Other power plants are available, such as two-cylinder fuel engines, miniature Wankel rotary engines, and miniature diesel engines. These are primarily novelty engines, to be tried out and enjoyed after the pleasures and problems associated with the more standard fuel engines have been experienced. One other type of driving force which has its attractions for boating modelists is the external combustion engine, the steam engine. Since its only R/C application is in boating, we'll look at it in our chapter on that subject.

Some R/C hobbyists start from scratch and build

engines of their own, finding as much enjoyment in this as they do with their R/C sporting. This requires a miniature machine shop, an item that can't be purchased off the shelf and put to work with no training in machine work. Few modelists have such a machine shop, but all modelists should have the space and tools that are needed to work on their little engines. Engines require their share of work, with that share determined by how much the hobbyist wants to get out of the engine.

The powered glider enthusiast expects no more of his .049 engine than for it to get his glider up in the air, where wind currents can then take over. This hobbyist may never do much more than change the glow plug as it wears out. The R/C car racer, on the other hand, needs to get every ounce of performance out of his engine when there's a World Championship at stake, and will probably tear down the engine and modify it before a big race.

Modifications can be—and certainly are—made to both electric and fuel-powered engines. These very effective modifications do not require anything more than a few hand tools and some guidance in using them. But before you start doing any modifying on any type of R/C model, master the workings of that model in its stock condition, and have a very specific route to travel on your way to improving its performance.

4

On the Tracks

Newspapers and magazines constantly mention Americans' love affair with the car. This love affair is not exclusively American, however. Throughout the world, people love old junker cars, shiny new ones, custom-builts, and all kinds of auto races.

Tens of thousands cheered when Carlos Reutterrman won the Grand Prix at Monaco, averaging 88 mph over the twisting, turning course. But that wasn't the only road race run at Monaco that day in 1978. Four thousand people filled the grandstand to overflowing as Phil Greeno won the first World Cup R/C Car Race at a scale speed that averaged over 300 mph on a course much shorter, but no less tough, than the course for the full-sized racers. Phil beat every American on the track.

Phil Greeno is from Great Britain. Debbie Preston, who dropped back to fifth place in the race because of car handling problems, but clawed her way back to second after her pit crew changed one of her tires, is also from Great Britain. Although the eight Americans who competed at Monaco were all U.S. National R/C car racing champs at one time or another, none of them was among the first ten finishers in the World Cup R/C Car Race.

There were some reasons for the poor showing of the Americans there. They had heating problems with their disc brakes because of the high speeds reached on the very long straightaway at Monaco, a problem which drivers from other countries had already solved because of their familiarity with the type of R/C car track set up at Monaco. The Americans weren't used to racing in the counterclockwise direction that's favored on R/C car racing tracks on the Continent. And while the European cars were outfitted with differential gears on their rear axles, the American cars still raced with solid rear axles. There were lots of excuses to be found, but the American drivers knew very well that their European competitors were simply into this particular kind of R/C racing more deeply than they.

Japanese race drivers were home racing their dune buggies, but drivers from Great Britain, Italy, and the Netherlands all did better with their little cars than did the Americans. However, American drivers and race cars are improving rapidly as R/C cars lead the way in the surging popularity of R/C sporting in this country. Our racers are burning up the existing tracks instead of building many new ones. U.S. drivers seem to be too busy enjoying the sport and in preparing themselves and their cars for the World Cup rematch in Switzerland, to go in search of new racing fans and car drivers.

Most American R/C car racing tracks aren't easy to

This ⅛ scale fuel powered race car comes complete off the
shelf, ready to race. (Courtesy Model Racing Products, Inc.)

find. Nevertheless, they draw more and more people to them each racing Sunday, for there are thrills and excitement for all at those tracks. Also, getting all the way into car racing is easier than getting all the way into racing R/C boats or planes. Some R/C airplanes and racing boats may cost less to set up and run, but the boats require a body of water, and the airplanes need wide open spaces and sometimes very painfully acquired skills. An R/C car, on the other hand, can be set up and run with a minimum of skills in building and driving, and the model can then be sent on its trial run in the driveway or on the street.

R/C cars are rugged and durable, made to stand a great deal of abuse. When an R/C driving mishap occurs, the car is usually none the worse for it while salvage operations are needed for the R/C boat, and the R/C airplane that crashed may call for a bushel basket. R/C cars are said to be gentler to the hands than the boat or plane, since there is not a spinning propeller to gouge a finger. There is, however, the danger of burning a finger on a hot engine and the danger of getting whacked in the ankle by five pounds of hurtling Lotus Can-Am. Also there's the danger of letting the smell of nitromethane and hot castor oil fumes go to your head so that you have to get out of the pits for fresh air.

There are advantages and disadvantages to every form of R/C sport. What attracts an individual to one form of the sport may be exactly what turns the next person away from it. In R/C racing the big attraction is the action. While other R/C racers do a lot of prerace talking and tinkering, the R/C car driver is out there racing on the track. If you want fast racing action right now, find a track close to you and start looking and learning.

As with any other form of R/C modeling, your local hobby shop is the place to begin. Its proprietor might be busy, he might not care a hoot about cars himself, but he will at least be able to direct you to the hobby shop person who is also a racing car driver or fan. There is a hobby shop proprietor in your city who has all the gear you need for R/C cars and can tell you where to go to put it to use. But look and learn at the hobby shop and at the track before you buy anything more than a magazine on the subject.

You may have seen the little plastic, electrically driven cars available in toy stores and hobby shops. These include semitrucks, tanks, and dune buggies. Although operated by radio control, they're capable of only very low speeds and are operable within only a few yards of their simple transmitters. The fully involved R/C race car driver would pass up these little things as mere toys. Yet it's fun to tool one of these toys around the legs of a coffee table or back it into a tough little parking place. While these don't provide the competition of yesterday's slot cars, they do represent some of the sophistication that has gone from computers and spaceships into recreational sports.

A giant step up from these little cars are the $^1/_{12}$ electric racing cars. Their chassis are engineered along the same lines as the larger $^1/_8$ scale fuel-powered racers, and their radio controls are the same. Although R/C racing cars are available in a variety of body styles, serious racers prefer the Can-Am body style because of its excellent aerodynamic shape. A $^1/_{12}$ electric race car can be had complete and ready to run, with radio gear included, for about two hundred dollars. The car can use either a four-cell or a six-cell battery pack. The four-battery cars clip along at about 22 mph, while the six-packer hits speeds of up to 30 mph as it comes from the dealer's shelf. These are the cars that conform to the specifications laid down by ROAR, the Radio-Operated Association of Racers.

Thirty mph translates to well over two hundred scale miles per hour, more than enough to keep you up on your toes and down off the top end of your throttle until you've mastered a few driving skills. These skills come through racing, and the cars are built to be raced. The electric cars are clean and free of the messy fuels, noise and engine starting problems that attract some people to the ⅛ cars. The electric cars are ideal for the driver who doesn't have the time or the inclination for anything more mechanical than changing a tire. Do not, however, rush out and buy one till you've checked on whether you'll be able to have any real fun with it beyond running it up and down your driveway.

Running a one-car race isn't very much fun. Before you get an R/C race car, find out for sure if there's a car racing club close to you and get involved with its races. There are plenty of things to do at the racing meets in addition to racing a car. Track stewards are needed at

A veteran of many races, this ⅛ R/C fuel car rests on its work bench with its plastic body removed. The wheel below it is driven by a full-sized car battery to kick over the engine in the racer.

every major turn in every race to pick up the overturned race cars and set them back down on their wheels. Lap counters are needed to keep the cars' racing order straight as they zip through the winding road-race-type course, or speed around the oval, weaving in and out of traffic jams, avoiding the pileups, lapping the slower cars.

You may be an antisocial sort, but in no time you'll be fully involved in the race, dodging cars, getting them back in the race, cheering a favorite on. More than in any other R/C sport, car racers are sociable and will go out of their way to help one another and any interested newcomer.

The Puget Sound Radio-Controlled Car Club (PSR/CCC) in Seattle is typical of the many good clubs around the country. It is sanctioned by ROAR and has about twenty to thirty club members at any one time. These currently include Tony Bellizi, seven times a National Champion; Bob Welch, two-time champ; and four others who are nationally rated R/C car drivers. Two young women and several boys under twelve years of age also race elbow to elbow with the name drivers. Half the club's drivers are under twenty-one and some are well past forty. All the club members are happy to pass on the racing tips they have at their disposal and are particularly happy when a newcomer from a distant neighborhood joins in, learns fast, and then departs the scene to start up a club that the PSR/CCC can compete against in a few months.

The racing arena for the PSR/CCC is the parking lot

at the Totem Lake Shopping Center. Membership fee is five dollars a year, and club members pay a dollar every racing Sunday, while nonmembers kick in two bucks to race. They money goes for trophies and an annual banquet. The club makes a few additional dollars by raffling off a racing car now and then to the crowd of spectators at their unusually visible location. Greg Sheehan, club president, helps draw those crowds with the good announcing job he does through the races. He and the races themselves have caused more than one shopper to tarry a while, win a car, and join the club.

On a racing Sunday the entries are filed with the chief steward, and qualifying times are recorded for the day as the veteran racers get the feel of the track and the novices try to better the practice runs they've made on the track that morning. Qualifying times are the criterion for the grouping of up to eight cars for each of the day's ten-lap heat races, so that the novice rarely meets the veteran in these shorter races.

Each driver has a pit crew consisting of one person, who assists at the start of the race and does whatever can be done in case of a breakdown on the track. Racers from other heats often serve in this capacity or as track stewards or lap counters. Six-cell electric race cars run on the outdoor tracks, and four-cell racers are used on the hardwood floors of a school gymnasium when bad weather prevents the club from racing outdoors.

When racing on hardwood, better traction is gained by painting a little silicone on the cars' tires. Most of the PSR/CCC's races, however, take place outside on asphalt with fuel-powered ⅛ scale cars. All of the races are quick and competitive, with the winners of the heat races qualifying for the longer main event race and the also-rans getting into one of perhaps several shorter semimains. Everyone who goes out with a car on a racing Sunday can be assured of getting into two races.

The new periodical *Racing Car World* says of this club: ''There is a great feeling of cooperation and comradeship amongst the racers, which is vital to everyone having a good time and putting on a good race, which they do.'' This could be applied to every R/C car club I have seen.

There are electric race cars and there are modified electric race cars. Mark Miranda started out with a four-cell electric racer when he was sixteen years old, quickly added two more batteries to race in the six-cell stock class, and then swiftly moved on to the modified competition. The club he was in raced on the second and fourth Sundays of every month in the parking lot of Ace Auto Parts in Lemon Grove, California.

Mark was fortunate. Right from the start, he did well. He had the sort of coordination it takes to remotely and yet very intimately guide a car over the unbanked track, pushing it hard at all times, right to the limit of spinning out on the 180-degree curves, going into the straight-away and braking into the turns, and at all times avoiding the spinouts and crack-ups that happen so quickly and frequently in novices' races.

Mark used the Futaba two-channel radio that most

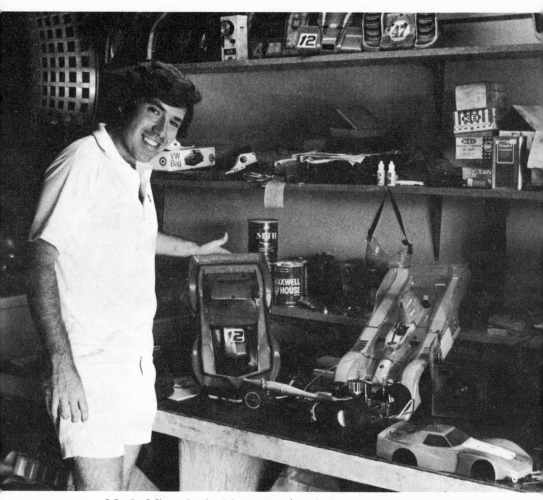

Mark Miranda in his garage/workshop, where he built up the cars that have turned him into a semi-pro R/C car racer.

American racers favor and, like most of them, he had a miniature steering wheel for direction and a slot-car-type pistol-grip throttle and brake control. Winning races came easily for Mark, and he got help from the veteran drivers in modifying his electric car.

The first modification most racers make is the simple expedient of changing the tires on the racing car. The trick comes in choosing the right kind of tire for the track on any given day. Harder, firmer tires provide the best traction on a dusty, slippery track, while softer tires are better on a clean, firm track. All the tires are solid rubber or synthetic rubber, and need no air to inflate them. The softer tires wear out quickly. Some of them won't last through a fifty-lap race. Some racers prefer softer tires on the larger diametered rear wheels, and others like it the other way around.

Either way, a new sort of racing fun starts with the modifications, because then the race driver must also become a mechanic and a racing car design engineer. This adds a whole new dimension to a hobbyist's pleasure as competitors are consulted and experiments made. Utter frustration or great exultation may be experienced as a newly modified car enters the competition on a racing Sunday.

Mark learned about the effects a tire can have on a race, and he put what he learned to work for him. He made weight distribution changes in his electric car, lowering its center of gravity. He rewound his electric motor, and again got better results on the track. Although the electric car doesn't lend itself to all the

The trackside scene at an R/C car race can be as frantic as that at Indy, as racers and pit crew change places from one race to the next.

modifications that may be made on a fuel-powered racer, Mark was already learning about the workshop tricks that would help him win ⅛ scale races, since the electric cars are in many ways the same as the fuelers.

Fuel or electric, the racing cars' steering linkage is simple and direct. A forward/reverse motor in the steering servo operates a rod that is linked by other rods to the car's front wheels. There are differences in the speed with which servos move, and race cars need quick acting servos for quick changes in direction.

The front wheels of the R/C racing car used to be spring-loaded, or even independently suspended, as in a full-sized racing car. Recently, however, the American racing car chassis makers found this suspension wasn't needed and that a softer ride actually slowed their cars down. Although the Monocan experience might change some design philosophies, American chassis manufacturers moved away from the complexity of copying a full-sized race car, so that now the only springy part of an R/C car's chassis is the fiberglass plate on which the chassis' functioning parts are attached. Unlike the old aluminum chassis, the fiberglass chassis allow the car to flex on the track while still keeping everything firmly in line. And the fiberglass chassis won't get bent out of shape by a nasty collision.

The rear end of an R/C race car is more complex than the front, allowing for much more innovation. Two control rods run from the throttling servo, one to either a rheostat on an electric car or a carburetor on a fueler, and the other to a disc brake, which is part of the rear axle. Since American cars have solid rear axles, both of the car's extra-wide rear tires rotate at the same speed, even in the tightest of turns. A driving gear as well as the disc brake is mounted on this rear axle. The gear, whose diameter is almost as large as a rear wheel, meshes directly with a gear on the motor's drive shaft, so these cars are direct drive, with no transmission. Between the gear and the motor, however, there is an automatic, centrifugal clutch. The clutch has two steel shoes that swing out and engage the gears and the motor as the motor speeds up, and which retract and allow the car to sit at idle at the starting line while the driver waits for the green flag. These are common arrangements for both electric and fuel-powered cars.

Modifications usually begin at the gears, but as gear ratios are changed to give the car more speed, the car becomes unstable at low speeds. That is, power pouring to the wheels at the start of a race will spin the car in a circle, burning rubber, instead of speeding away down the track. To give it more stability on the starts, pieces are cut out of the clutch shoes, allowing the clutch to slip for the few instants it takes to get the car in motion.

Mark made the gear and clutch changes on his electric car and, as mentioned, rewired its motor. By using smaller wire with fewer turns on the armature, he got higher speed out of his motor. This rewiring appreciably shortened the life of his motor, but costs such as these are to be expected when there's room for another trophy on the mantelpiece. Mark garnered his share of trophies. While he still races his modified electric car on occasion, the smell of castor oil and nitro and the snarlings of eight hot racers drew him on into the full dimension of R/C car racing, the ⅛ Modified Gas races.

He didn't spend a lot of time racing ⅛ stock cars. He got the feel for the much faster cars, more than twice as fast as the electrics, and obtained the auxiliary equipment needed to race with fuel. More spare parts are required at trackside for these more powerful and more complex cars, and an electric starter is necessary for their engines.

Most racers have collapsible workbenches, which they set up next to the opened hood of their passenger cars. The electric starter is built into the workbench. It's just a small motor, driven by the big car's battery, which turns a rubber wheel sticking up out of the table top. The racing car's clutch housing is held against the rubber wheel to start up the engine, with the one-and-one-half-volt dry cell battery lighting up the glow plug in the racer's engine. A good workbench and a good pit crewman are necessary to win races. Engine modifications help, but not so much as they used to.

Most racers used to run a Veco .19 in their cars. It's a very good engine, but it was designed for airplane use originally. Drivers need more power, more speed than the stock Veco .19 could provide, and the drivers in Mark's club told him how to modify his Veco.

First Mark replaced the cylinder head on his engine with a high-compression head, which he bought at his local hobby store. He then advanced the engine's timing and streamlined its inner workings in the process. Engine timing is done with the ignition system in full-sized four-cycle cars. On a two-cycle glow-plug model car, which has no ignition system, it's done by enlarging the intake and exhaust ports in the cylinder and in the crankshaft. Mark ground and cut metal from the crankshaft, the fuel and exhaust ports, the piston, and he also filled in any sharp engine recesses with metal-filled epoxy. He didn't know a thing about engines when he started, but with guidance from drivers such as Bill Jianis, another National Champion, Mark did the work with hand tools—and he did it well. Now Mark can strip down his motor and make necessary repairs on his workbench between races, although his new engine doesn't require the custom work that went into his Veco.

Mark runs a K & B .21 now, an engine designed for R/C race cars. It's the largest displacement allowed under ROAR racing rules, and so far these new engines have needed no modifications beyond their carburetion. Larger Perry carburetors are installed on the K & B engines, and more nitromethane is added to the fuel. The K & B is a hot little engine in its stock condition, and now K & B are the people who are working on internal modifications to make it hotter.

Mark is working on an external modification. He has installed a tuned muffler, which increases his compression ratio and gives him a higher top end, at the same time giving him better throttle control at low speeds. Mark, twenty-one now, gets mufflers and parts at a substantial discount since he became a semiprofessional race car driver.

A few drivers, like Bill Jianis, are members of Team Associated Electric. Associated Electric makes the most widely accepted competition cars, and they use drivers like Bill to test out their latest factory developments and provide them with feedback from neighborhood tracks. Bill was one of the American drivers sent to Monaco, with all expenses paid. There aren't many pros like Bill Jianis, but there are a great many semipros like Mark. Having proved himself on the tracks, and eventually knowing more about R/C racing cars than the proprietor of his hobby shop, Mark was hired to work there. He's going to college at night now, is racing every other Sunday, and hopes he'll find a way to get to the World Cup races next year.

It was a pleasure to watch Mark race at the last meeting of the San Diego R/C Racing Car Association. Club members and others met at the parking lot of Local 542 Teamster's Union Hall, where an excellent course has been laid out on the asphalt. Mark did some practice runs with his newly tuned muffler and made some tire changes because of the dusty track condition. His qualifying time was better than that of his brother, Lee, a newcomer to the sport, so the brothers were placed in different heat races, allowing each to pit for the other. The guardrails were set up, lap counters and timers were picked from the volunteers, and as the racers made last minute preparations, Mark helped out with work and his experience.

Hal Empey, who had raced only a few times, and was enthused and excited, was running lap after practice lap and making adjustments on his car. When Hal's car broke down, Mark helped him get it back together and gave him some Loctite. Vibration on these little cars is terrific; without a lubricant like Loctite on nuts and bolts, cars vibrate to pieces on the track. Hal, a taxicab dispatcher, enjoys being able to forget about the big cars by racing the little ones on Sundays. He is also a veteran R/C airplane pilot, but he says, "I don't fly since I got into cars. After nine months of building went into my last airplane, and I watched as it crashed, I tried car racing. It's great. There's more action in this than in any other kind of R/C."

It was Larry Thomas's first time at the track with the new car he had designed and built himself. Larry had been deeply involved with full-sized stock car racing for twelve years, both as driver and a mechanic. He said, "I'm through with that. This is more relaxing and a whole lot more fun."

Lee and Hal did better than they ever had that day. Larry trailed the field in his heat race, until his was the last car on the track and still spinning out on the curves. But Larry was smiling and nodding as he picked up his car, saying, "I know what's wrong with it now."

Mark got off to a bad start. His engine stalled at the green flag. Lee grabbed up Mark's car and ran to their workbench, fired up the car and took it back to the starting line, from which Mark took off a full lap behind the others. Mark placed second in his heat race, which gave him a spot in the main event. There he got a better feel for his new tuned muffler as he took another first and got some more points in the ROAR standings.

After the races, the club members discussed the much bigger racing day that was scheduled for the following Sunday at Anaheim. They were going up in a group, with several cars, and while these arrangements were being made, Mark said, "I don't know when I'm going to find time to race it, but I'm building an R/C racing sailboat now. I don't know a thing about sailing, but I've wanted to learn for a long time."

Mark will learn a great deal about sailing and surely do well at his new R/C hobby. And perhaps when he goes to the World Cup R/C Car Races next year at Geneva, he'll take his sailboat along.

Track stewards and pit crew rush to set things in order after a jam-up on the track—and the race still roars on.

5

On the Water

About the only kind of boat you will not see on an R/C yachting pond is a miniature Indian birchbark canoe. The rest are all there, from galley slave boats with working oars to submersible submarines, from screaming hydroplanes that race around marker buoys to clean-lined reproductions of the 12-meter racing sloops that compete for the America's Cup. The miniature world of R/C boating is rich in variety, with plenty of room for a faster or better boat.

The fastest boats are, of course, the racing speedboats. These provide the fastest action and most thrills on the water. R/C speedboating has many similarities to R/C car racing. Yet it also has some distinct differences and challenges not to be found with the four-wheeled competitive speedsters.

Unlike cars, there is a choice of hull shapes in boat racing, with modelists about equally divided in their preferences for the deep vee, or monoplane hull, and the hydroplane hull shape. The monoplane hull is smooth all the way, with no discontinuities or steps along its wetted surface. This kind of hull has the traditional keel. It's easier to handle than is the hydroplane hull. The boat with the monoplane hull may also be referred to as an offshore racing boat, since it's copied from the full-sized speedboats that race for hundreds of miles over the open sea. It is a hull shape that can race very well on a pond that is too choppy for the somewhat faster and more skittish hydroplane.

The hydroplane has a step or some sort of concavity in its hull which gives it very decided airfoil characteristics. At times the only portions of a hydroplane touching the water is its screw and rudder. It is this great reduction in friction between boat and water that allows the hydroplane to operate at such terrific speeds. The monoplane hull can depart from the water at high speeds, too, though this type of hull can't remain airborne for as long as the hydroplane.

As with cars, the racing speedboat modelist has a choice of fuel or electric drive. The North American Model Boat Association (NAMBA) works with the International Model Power Boat Association (IMPBA), in establishing the various speedboating classes, so that a skillful race with a small boat won't be blown out of the water by the sheer power of the competitor with a monstrous big motor.

Electric drive, of course, is cleaner and easier than fuel drive. Weight considerations are not such a large factor with boats, so the electric speedboat can use the heavier, longer-lasting lead-sulfate-type battery which wouldn't fit into an electric racing car. The gas-powered speedboat is faster and satisfyingly noisier, but has the disadvantages of fuel handling, balky engine starting even with the help of an electric starter, and the fine tuning of the screaming engine in the short time allowed under boat racing rules. Disadvantages? These are the very factors that draw the modelist to the gas-powered racer. These bring about the same sort of franzied hassles suffered through and overcome by the racers who risk their lives in 2,000-horsepower Thunderboats. The fuel-powered racer provides more racing realism than does the electric—and it also provides for more speed.

A hydroplane with a .60 motor in it will hit speeds of up to 60 mph, the scaled-up equivalent of a full-sized boat doing 400 mph. This isn't at all easy to handle during the course of a twenty-lap race, and this is where the racing boat sport takes a significant departure from the sport of racing cars.

When an R/C racing car overturns on a track, which is often, it frequently rights itself and keeps on running in the race with no more than some scratches on its body and the loss of a few seconds' running time. It's not uncommon for a racer to roll his car in a way that would demolish a full-sized car and its driver, and then go on to place first in the event. Also, there's always a race steward at hand to dart out and right the car that's turned turtle and stayed right there with its wheels pointing up in the air. Not so with a racing speedboat. The R/C boat racer may injure nothing more than his personal pride when some careless handling capsizes

A deep-vee hull racing boat, powered by a hot .40 cubic inch engine: glossy, bright, and ready to run in the next heat race.

the boat, and the boat may not be damaged at all, but when a mistake turns a boat on its back that boat is out of the race.

This sort of racing takes a great deal of skill. It takes more care in handling than the car racer is used to exercising. It provides for a certain degree of realism that is lacking in racing R/C cars. And, since a crash on the water does not leave the scars made by tumbling on asphalt, it also allows the racing boat modelist to do some very excellent detail work on the hull.

Model racing boats are invariably beautifully finished and realistically decorated with racing designs and insignias. Model boaters, in general, lean much more toward this sort of meticulous detail work than do other modelists. In the case of the racing boat, there's a practical reason for getting a glasslike finish on the hull. It is drag—friction between water and hull—that holds a boat back. So a smooth and glassy finish on the hull can add several miles per hour to a boat's performance. Beyond the strictly practical considerations, there is real aesthetic consideration involved with the smoothly finished and nicely decorated boat. There is more to building a boat than there is to building a car.

Some racing hulls are made of fiberglass and some of wood sheeting. Decking and subdecking and frames and struts are made of spruce and mahogany and birch plywood. The construction of a model boat kit is much like the construction of a real speedboat. It is typically built upside down on a board, which insures that the hull will be straight and true. The subdecking is pinned to the board, and glue or quick-setting epoxy resin is used to attach the frames. The keel and the chine stringers are cemented on when the frame's glue has set. The hull is then laid or built over this. The boat is removed from the board for the decking to be laid on. With epoxy coatings and modeler's paint, the glossy, glassy hull finish is achieved, then the motor and controls are installed.

Building a boat kit doesn't take many special tools. Clamps are a very handy item to have around during the building. And after it's been built an inexpensive, aerosol-operated airbrush is very good for doing the finishing work.

Just a few years ago, engines in gas-powered speedboats were modified model airplane engines, with the major modification being the addition of a cooling jacket. Most of these cooling jackets were homemade affairs, and lots of those modified airplane engines are still running racing boats. But now there is more and more modeling equipment available which has been designed and made expressly for the model speedboater.

The Kool-Klamp is one piece of this equipment. It's a hollow band that fits closely around the air-cooling fins of the cylinder head of an engine. A tube set in the wake of the boat's screw picks up water, which circulates through the Kool-Klamp, effectively cooling the engine before being discharged from the boat through another tube. Engines with built-in cooling jackets that work on this same principle go into many of the new boats. Beautiful little outboard motors are made for adding still more realism to the racing boat, and for making the boat more maneuverable. Boat kits are abundant, in all forms and shapes, with Dumas Products, Inc. being one of the leaders in the field. Tiny marine engines are coming out in ever wider varieties now, as are some fascinating mechanical accessories.

One new and very welcome piece of equipment, which will certainly find its way into a great many fuel-powered R/C racing boats, is a device called the

Lectra-Start. A three-channel radio is needed to operate a boat with the Lectra-Start. One channel operates the rudder, the second operates the throttle, and the third goes to switch on the electric motor mounted inboard next to the boat's engine. The Lectra-Start can be used to fire up an engine that stalls during a race. It also adds one more classy little touch of racing realism.

The sleek, brightly colored hydroplane sits hull down in the water. Its miniature driver, helmeted and wearing a life preserver, sits quietly gripping the steering wheel while the rest of the boats in the race are fired up and hustled on down to the water. When the other boats are in the water and jockeying for their starting positions in the race, our hydroplane's Lectra-Started motor fires up with a puff of smoke and a roar, then smoothly joins the rest of the pack, ready to run a good race.

The start of a speedboat race is an exciting and closely regulated affair. The course on our local R/C boating pond is an oval one, with two parallel straightaways just over one hundred yards long, joined by two sweeping, thirty-foot radius curves. The course is marked off with buoys. The start and finish line is halfway down one of the straightaways, directly in front of the judges' stand. The stand is flanked on each side with a starting pit, where the action begins at race time. A starting clock is in view of all racers, marking off thirty seconds with each sweep of its large hand.

Two minutes of pit time is allowed for the modeler to start the engine and launch and release his boat. When pit time is over, clock time begins. Now each racer has thirty seconds to move his boat through a designated milling pattern as the crafts approach the starting line. Throttles are opened and engines roar as the boats hurtle down the course. Any boat that jumps the start is disqualified. The rest of the pack screams into the first turn throwing up rooster tails and spewing out wakes as they go. Six laps of careful handling and all-out racing effort are needed to complete a heat race. The top finishers go on to the main event and win the congratulations of fans and competitors, while the racer who was crossed up in the wakes of the other boats rows the dinghy to his capsized craft. As he rows, he hopes he has adequately waterproofed his radio gear and servos.

If you feel that speedboat racing is your sort of R/C sport, check first to make sure there are other enthusiasts in your community, then start out with a simple kit boat. It's best to start out with a small kit and a small motor.

The smallest gas engines belong in the ½A class, where the .049 engine is the favorite. Class A includes all engines up to and including the .21 displacement. Class B goes up to .45 cubic inches, Class C to .67, and Class X includes engines up to a whopping 1.34 cubic inches displacement. That is a lot of engine for a model boat. Some modelists go for one big engine, others go for more than one, and race in a class where two or three engines sling their boats through the water, just like the rough-water speedboats that race on the open seas.

There are R/C boat modelists who scorn all that power and rely on the wind for their weekend racing competition. Promptly at noon at our local model yacht basin, the speedboaters gather up their paraphernalia and make way for the stately ladies of the sea. "Rag sailors," the speedboaters mutter, as the racing sloops are launched. "Stink-potters," say the sailboaters, as sails are set and streamlined hulls hiss quietly through the water.

Building and operating a sailboat is said to be more demanding than doing the same with an R/C speedboat. This is not really true. It does take more time to build a sailboat kit, it does take a three-channel radio to operate one really right, and indeed they are tricky to sail. But as far as the R/C sailboaters are concerned, tinkering with a little gas engine would be far more demanding than building a model sloop. Herein lies the very widespread appeal of R/C modeling—various facets of the sport hold deep fascination for various people.

The R/C sailboater is usually an experienced sailor. He may have a forty-foot sloop of his own, tied up at the mooring he passes on his way to the model yacht basin, where he can experience all the pleasures of sailing in the time it takes to get the full-sized boat under way. Or he may have given up full-sized sailing for some reason, but still craves the fun of sailing. Many other sailboaters have never owned a full-sized boat and never will, yet enjoy all the knowledge and skills of yachtsmen on the scaled-down size of the R/C world.

All R/C sailboaters know the points of sailing before they launch their boats. Books abound on the subject of sailing. If you feel that R/C sailing may be right for you,

Stately R/C racing sloops glide through the water in regal
fashion while their on-shore skippers gleefully use every dirty
trick possible to win the race.

obtain a book about how to sail and learn from paper before you try it on water. Learn nautical nomenclature. Building a model sailboat is not easy, even when you know the terminology. The plans in a sailboat kit are written in nautical terms, and the beginner may have trouble in such things as attaching the clew to the foot.

It takes 100 to 150 hours of modeling work to put together a good, big racing sailboat. Then, sailing the boat is quite a departure from turning a steering wheel, working a throttle, and complacently relying on a motor to make the boat move toward a destination. Although the sailing vessel has been highly refined through the centuries, it still remains a primitive form of conveyance, with the sailor still at the mercy of the wind. A sailor out on the bay in his little Sabot might be dozing as the breeze wafts him on toward his destination, but his hand on the tiller tells him just how much water pressure there is on the hull of the boat, and his hand on the mainsheet tells him how to balance the lateral water pressure with pressure from the breeze.

The R/C sailboater can't feel those pressures. He has to look for them from many yards away, noting every smallest movement of the boat and compensating for them all with movements of electronic levers. And in R/C sailing, the R/Cer encounters the seemingly simple problem of left and right.

At least it sounds like a simple problem, and indeed it is fairly simple for the R/C car driver and speedboater. The problem is this: As the radio-controlled model is moving away from you, moving the steering lever to the right will make the model move to your right. But as the same model is moving toward you, the same lever movement and rudder movement—to the right—will make the model move to your left. The modelist has to mentally place himself inside the model to steer it correctly.

Obviously this isn't much of a problem for the model car and speedboat racer, primarily because those models are moving on a closed course. But the buoys that mark the course for a racing sailboat are more randomly placed, and the sailboat must go with the wind, tacking and jibing, changing direction, ever in search of a breeze from just the right angle. This left-right orientation, this placement of the sailor in the cockpit of the boat, takes some getting used to. Indeed, the fully experienced sailor can have more trouble mastering this than does the beginner. (When it comes to flying an R/C airplane, the left-right confusion also requires a lot of practice.)

Dumas Boats and Sterling Models and others make excellent racing sailboat kits. Like speedboat models, model sailboats are built to compete in classes. These include the 50/800 class, the 36/600 class, the soling classes, the popular 6- and 12-meter classes, and others. Unlike model speedboats, however, the model racing sailboat is not a faithful reproduction of an existing, successful, full-sized racing boat. Sailboating aerodynamics exert different effects as a 12-meter boat is reduced in size to one-meter long. The same ten-knot breeze that briskly moves the *America* through the water comes on to the miniature sailboat as a howling gale. The sails on a miniature boat are therefore appreciably narrower than true scale, and hull design undergoes subtle changes in the miniaturization.

Boats in these classes must all conform to rigid specifications in their dimensions, sail areas, and weights. This equality in dimensions once again makes a sailboat race primarily a test of the sailor's skills, although some R/C sailboaters secretly boast of finding an edge over the competition by judicious distribution of the weight allowed for their class of sailboat. Most of the weight goes into the keel, but it can be distributed fore or aft. This heavy keel makes it almost impossible for the racing sailboat to capsize, but racing sailboats can ship water, so their radio equipment must be waterproofed.

One servo operates the sailboat's rudder, a second its mainsail, and if a third is available it operates the boat's jib sail. Sailboats can get along without the jib-sail control at the expense of losing only a little racing speed. The servo that operates the mainsail is special to sailboating. It takes the place of the powerful winch on a full-sized sailboat that hauls in dozens of square yards of sail against the pressure of the wind. The R/C servo can be a miniaturized winch or it may be a strong little servo fitted out with a lever arm that moves the sail quickly against a wind force of up to fifty pounds on the miniature sail. The mast and sail on these boats are removable for ease in transporting the craft to the yacht basin.

R/C sailboaters don't seem to worry about any of these matters when they're racing. Transmitters in hand, they stroll along the shoreline, some sloshing along through ankle-deep water, most kibitzing back and forth, and all using every dirty trick known in sailboating circles. Stealing the wind is a favorite trick. If one sailboat can be maneuvered close on the windward side of another, the second boat gets only the turbulent leavings of the wind that spills out of the first boat's sails. And the experienced sailor can always make it difficult for a challenger to pass between the marker buoy and the leading boat.

Judges are in the stands, immune to the kibitzing, closely watching to see that the dirty tricks all fall within the boundaries of racing club rules. An R/C sailboating race looks like a jolly, relaxed affair. But there is a lot of good-natured infighting all through a race. No one really relaxes until the boats cross the finish line and the winner claims the trophy.

Some R/C racing sailboaters never win a trophy. Ralph McConnel was one of these. He built a beautiful *Equation* from a kit to race in the 36/600 class. Having had some experience with building balsa and tissue model airplanes, Ralph did a superlative job on his first model boat. And as he was building the model, he was saving his money for a three-channel radio, which he duly purchased and put in his boat. Ralph had had some sailing experience, and could soon sail his boat around the basin. But he couldn't win a race. He didn't know why, but after a couple of dozen close races, he still

This very fast R/C hydroplane was built from plans that were nothing more than pictures of its full-sized prototype.

hadn't crossed the finish line first. He had had a good deal of fun racing his boat, he had made some new friends, but he hadn't won any trophies, and that didn't set well with him.

On reflection, it seemed to him that the bulk of his pleasures in R/C sailboating had come from building the boat to begin with, so Ralph sold his *Equation* to someone less talented at building than he and entered another world of R/C boating—scale modeling.

Ralph won some tropies and blue ribbons here, for scale modeling is the realm of the painstaking craftsman. Scale-model ships and boats are show boats. They are very workable show boats because of the radio gear in them, but they're not built for speed as are the racing boats. They are built to exercise dextrous fingers and ingenious minds. Like many beginning scale modelers, Ralph started out with a scale-model tugboat kit. He did a fine job at it. He won some prizes at hobby shows with it and still receives a great deal of admiration each time he gives his boat a workout in the bay. He added to it, installing an automobile windshield washer pump as a replica of the surge pumps that full-sized tugs use for maneuvering.

Now Ralph is working on a Roman bireme, the ancient vessel that slaves propelled with two banks of oars on each side of the ship. This is a particularly challenging project for Ralph, since he is building it from drawings he found at the library. He carves and fits and sands each piece of wood as he goes. By using some worm gears he found in a model train shop, he has managed to get his thirty-six oars working together at a realistic speed. This realistic speed is quite important, since scale-model judges mark down the perfectly detailed ship that can move any faster than scale speed.

This is the kind of competition Ralph likes, and he's far from being alone in his hobby. Locally, the members of the Ship Modeler's Guild meet one night each month to talk over their projects and exchange ideas about model ships and boats. They frequently meet at shows and at the yacht basin and at public swimming pools to show off their craftsmanship and artistic talents to the interested public.

Al Lheroux has a fleet of warships, the largest of which is a six-foot long version of the battleship *Missouri*. His mini-*Missouri* maneuvers like its cumbersome prototype. Its radome slowly rotates. Its gun turrets slowly swivel and aim as the tape-recorded sounds of a naval battle can be heard coming up from its lower decks. Smoke puffs from the guns as blanks are fired, and if Al is in the right mood, his *Missouri* lays down a smoke screen as it takes off at flank speed.

Fascinated with the possibilities of radio control, Phil Headley bought and built an R/C airplane kit. He did such a good job on it that he couldn't stand the thought of it plowing into a tree. He, too, turned to scale-model shipbuilding. His current pride and joy is a World War II submarine of the *Balio* class.

Phil's sub cleaves through the water at just the right speed, either surfaced or submerged. And, either surfaced or submerged, it fires scale torpedoes at the touch of an onshore button. Phil built his miniature warship from scratch, as did Al Lheroux, and both exercised great ingenuity in doing so. For example, instead of using an impossibly tiny compressor to blow his sub's tanks and make it surface, Phil uses little tanks of liquid Freon,™ which turns into gas to blow the sub's tanks when a servo-operated valve is opened. Al used a conglomeration of pumps and motors and electrical relays in his *Missouri* to keep its costs down so he could add other vessels to his fleet.

A well made R/C scale model, like this reproduction of an historic San Francisco Scow Schooner, draws a crowd of admirers before it can be launched to go through its paces.

Phil Headley's submarine dives and surfaces on radioed commands, fires scale-size torpedoes, and has a device that will blow down its tanks and make it rise to the surface in the event of unexpected battery failure.

Phil Headley does his part in an R/C model boat demonstration with the submarine he built.

Dick Rice got some help from his wife in building a four-foot long model of an obscure vessel known as a San Francisco scow schooner. It has squatty, ungainly lines, but it's beautiful. He has documentation and old photographs to prove that the scow schooner actually existed, a requisite for it to be judged in a scale-model ship show. Dick used eight hundred feet of door trimming scrap he got from his carpenter neighbor to build the ship's hull and decks. He carved his ship's masts from the eucalyptus saplings that grow in his backyard. His wife, Bing, sews the sails and helps with the rigging, and they work on their hobby quite well together.

Tim Grabner got into old-fashioned workboats. In-spired by an article in *Model Ships and Boats*, a bimonthly magazine devoted to the boating hobby, he built a complete, working steam engine for his little tugboat.

Steam is the alternate form of driving force for boats that we mentioned before. It is cumbersome and old-fashioned, but it is an elegant form of propulsion for a realistically old-fashioned boat. Stewart Engines and Saito make both steam engine kits that can be assem-bled and complete steam engines for the steam engine fan. They are brass-bound and very well done, and can be fitted with a little steam whistle. Their boilers are most conveniently fired with bottled propane gas, since employing a miniature coal stoker is a little too much to expect from even the most ardent modelist. But some of these little steamboats contain the figurine of a helmsman with one movable hand on the tiller and the other on the remotely operated steam whistle.

Clearly, such boats as these are not for the beginner. Each, however, may represent a goal to shoot for as the on-the-water hobbyist plays and works in the miniature maritime world of R/C.

6

Preflight Training

Whatever type of R/C modeling and sporting you start into, don't try to get all the way into it too quickly. This is especially true when it comes to R/C flying. Do not follow in the footsteps of so many other aspiring R/C pilots and immediately dump four hundred dollars into a multichannel radio and a high-powered airplane. These often are people who become totally disenchanted with the whole idea of R/C sports within a few months.

Airplane kits aren't that easy to build, and this is particularly true of the larger ones. It takes some acquired skills and some patience to build one correctly, and having that expensive radio gear sitting quietly on the shelf does not add to the aspiring flier's patience. By the time the model is finished, the pilot is dying to fly it. It looks so sturdy and easy to fly that the would-be pilot thinks the skill can be mastered in no time.

It's true that some R/C models are relatively easy to fly. Some airplanes built from kits, properly put together and properly balanced, will fly by themselves when their radio controls are set at neutral. But others have to be flown every second they're in the air. Simply making an airplane execute a simple turn with no loss of altitude takes some skill and understanding about flying. And the novice's takeoffs and landings can range from a harrowing experience to a totally destructive one. However, anything can be mastered if it is approached slowly and intelligently.

They fly in the football stadium parking lot in the city where I live. I went down there one recent Saturday morning to watch. A young man of seventeen had a rather sedate-looking high-winged monoplane, which he took off from the asphalt and proceeded to put through a truly incredible series of stunts. He did hammerhead stalls and Cuban eights, all sorts of loops and breathtaking spins before smoothly landing the plane and taxiing it to a halt at his feet.

I asked him about his hobby, and he said he'd been into R/C flying for about a year. He had had about two months of weekend instruction from members of the local power flying club while flying the training airplane he had built from a kit. With the basics behind him, he went on to learn from other experts about doing some stunting, and he also developed some stunting techniques himself. In the tradition of R/C flying modelists, he passed on what he knew to another novice in the sport, a man who happened to be a very experienced commercial pilot.

The pilot had been surprised at how long it had taken him to master a little model airplane. One of his problems was that the radio control levers had no feel to them. When he pulled back on the stick that controlled the elevators, for instance, he felt none of the airspeed resistance he normally encountered when he performed that maneuver in a full-sized airplane. The commercial pilot, like most other novice R/C pilots, started off with a severe tendency to overcontrol his model airplane. And he had a particularly hard time with the left-right orientation business we discussed in regard to R/C sailboats.

But the young man was a patient teacher and the pilot a good student. The pilot had gone through full-sized flight training and was thoroughly indoctrinated with the knowledge that a mistake in the air can be fatal. Eventually he learned how to fly R/C planes as well as he flew full-sizes ones because both he and his teacher were patient.

While the young man and I were talking, another airplane taxied out on the asphalt. It was sleek and red and racy, but from the way it wavered about on its takeoff, there obviously wasn't a very experienced pilot at its controls. The airplane took off, made a properly slow turn to the left, and crashed head-on into a light standard. Its owner walked over and picked up the pieces of the plane and the shattered engine, then silently put them in his car and drove off with a dour expression. It's doubtful if he ever repaired his model. He had tried to go too far too fast.

R/C sporting is a hobby that can last a lifetime, so there's no reason to rush into it all at once. In any kind of R/C modeling and sporting, your progress must be limited by your pocketbook, your patience, and your skills as a craftsman. Start out on a small, simple scale and work slowly up to whatever your personal limits might be.

You can begin on a level which will all but dispense with any need to be a craftsman. There are very flyable kits available that can be put together and flown in a day. There is nothing at all wrong with these kits as learning tools that can offer a great deal of flying fun, but by staying entirely with such kits the R/C flier is limited on both ends of the R/C flying and modeling experience. This kind of R/C pilot doesn't know about the little complexities of building a simple airplane, and therefore can't build a really complex one. This kind of pilot does not get the R/C preflight training that can be had at a cost of only a few dollars and many hours of constructively active fun.

One way to start out is on a Peanut Scale. Buy a copy of *Model Builder* magazine, and while you're being greatly impressed by some of the things being done by modelists more advanced than you, look for an advertisement by Peck Polymers of La Mesa, California. Write them for a catalog or check at your local hobby store for Peanut Scale model airplane kits. The kits start at a dollar and go up to about fifteen. The one dollar kits are for planes powered by rubber bands. Intermediate models are powered with tiny carbon-dioxide-driven motors, and the most expensive are capable of handling those new, highly miniaturized servos. All the kits are of balsa wood and tissue paper and are reminiscent of bygone days.

Start with a one or two dollar kit and figure on spending a like amount for glue, straight pins, and a small Exacto knife. These are the basic tools for the airplane modelist. Get some waxed paper from the kitchen and start to work, carefully following the plans, learning about the problems of putting balsa wood sticks together to make an airframe, and covering the airframe with tissue paper so the model has airfoil surfaces. You will come up with an exceedingly light and delicate, yet surprisingly sturdy, model airplane.

What you've made is only powered by a rubber band, but it is more than a toy. It will really fly, and while it has no movable control surfaces other than its propeller, it operates under exactly the same forces of lift, gravity, thrust, and drag that govern the flights of full-sized airplanes.

A large and growing number of people are getting involved with rubber-band-powered airplanes. Some of these people are former R/C enthusiasts who grew tired of the expense, the paraphernalia, and the trips to wide open spaces needed for most types of R/C flying. These Peanut Scale planes can stay aloft for maybe a minute, so they can be quietly flown in an empty parking lot, on a quiet street, in a park, or in your backyard.

A Peanut Flying Club meets and flies in school gymnasiums in San Diego, where the vagaries of the wind won't interfere with their endurance competitions. There may be a club near you. The aviation editor

That old and almost forgotten plastic U-control plane can be salvaged for use in many ways in the small world of R/C.

of *Yankee Magazine* will tell you more about rubber-powered model airplanes and their clubs and pilots if you send him a stamped, self-addressed envelope at Dublin, New Hampshire 03444. You might get so interested in these little things that you'll never go on into radio control. But then again, you might want to have a model airplane you can keep up in the air for hours on end, looping and soaring, or you might want to hear the motor of your model airplane singing a snarling song as it rips past you at almost ground level.

If it's noise and speed and stunting at low levels that appeals to you, you can pause on the way to R/C and get into U-control flying. But do not get into U-control with one of those all-plastic ready-to-fly planes to be found in toy departments. These airplanes look good but fly like bricks, and are responsible for turning great numbers of people away from model flying forever. Of the myriads of these plastic U-control planes that have been sold, the majority made only one very unsatisfactory flight before being stuck in the back of the closet.

Build your own balsa and fabric U-control plane from a kit. These kits are usually easier to build than the Peanut Scale kits. Start out with a small one, a plane that will fly with no more than a .049 gas engine. The engine, complete with recoil starter and built-in gas tank, should cost less than ten dollars. A pint can of fuel, the dry cell battery for the engine's glow plug, a nylon propeller, and the U-controls may add up to another seven or eight dollars. With the experience you've gained from your Peanut Scale model, building the U-control plane will be a snap. But don't try to fly it the first time by yourself. Find an experienced U-controller to take your airplane off the ground for you, to tell you not to overcontrol it before he hands the controls over to you, and then to land it for you for that first time out.

The hobby shop proprietor will tell you where the U-controllers go to fly. You'll be able to hear them when you get close, because some of them fly very powerful planes. At a local U-control hangout in San Diego, Felipe Sanders flies a plane that he designed and built himself. It's powered by a .40 engine and souped up with a mixture very rich in nitromethane. Felipe's U-control plane has been clocked at 118 mph. He flies a somewhat slower U-control plane for air-to-air combat competition there at the park, trying to cut a paper streamer from the tail of another U-control plane before his paper streamer is cut by the other's propeller—and before a midair collision occurs.

Cy Steele is usually at the U-control hangout on weekends, enjoying himself as he teaches his kids how to fly and maintain their planes. U-control flying is primarily for the Steele family kids. For himself, Cy is building quite a large model of a two-engine B-25 World War II bomber. It will be controlled by the radio gear that his friend, Larry Young, is building from scratch.

You can pick up a lot about radio-controlled modeling if you get into U-control flying. While you're at your U-control flying, you might accidentally learn a few things about the motors that will fly your R/C airplane. More importantly, you'll certainly learn some valuable lessons about the importance of airspeed in flying.

Unlike a car or a boat, an airplane won't make any progress at all at low speeds. You've got to take off and fly an airplane at a good, brisk speed every time you fly one, including the first time. This is true for the R/C plane, the U-control plane, the Peanut Scale plane— and the supersonic Concorde. The third dimension of flying is the vertical dimension, and if an airplane is not getting enough lift from its airfoil surfaces, the direction it chooses to take in the third dimension is vertically down. If you try to go too slowly and cautiously with an airplane, it will stall in the air. Its tail will sag downward, its nose strain upward, and then it will fall back through the air and head nose-first for the ground.

The elevators are the control surfaces that make an airplane go up and down at proper airspeed. These are the control surfaces that can prevent a stall, and these are the only control surfaces that U-control airplanes have. All the stunting done by a U-control plane comes from changes in the position of its elevators. Felipe Sanders can stunt his U-control plane without any fear of stalling, because the motor on his plane is so powerful it will pull the plane straight up and out of a stall before the stall can occur.

But all those people who bought the all-plastic U-control planes at toy stores didn't have that sort of power. They didn't know about airspeed and power, because all it said on the box was that the airplane was ready to fly. So, if they got the underpowered airplane off the ground at all with its brand new motor, the airplane was just barely up to a safe airspeed. The neophyte fliers did the natural thing and tried to get the nose of the airplane up higher as they flew it at a nice, slow speed. Flying machines, however, are not at all natural. The natural thing was exactly the wrong thing to do. As the nose came up in response to the U-control lines, airspeed dropped below stalling speed, and the airplane hung in the air for a moment before nosing over and crashing nose-first into the ground. Those people might be flying hobbyists today if they had known enough to point the airplane down into a shallow dive to gain some airspeed and thus gain some control during their flight.

Airspeed and altitude are the two most important factors in keeping a plane in the air. If your airplane starts to lose airspeed, do the unnatural thing and point its nose downward. Only then can it pick up the airspeed it needs to allow its airfoils to start lifting again, so that it can climb back and gain the altitude you gave up in order to gain some control over the plane. If you wait too long to get the nose down and gain that airspeed, however, the stall cannot be prevented.

With this in mind, you might even get that wrecked plastic plane out of the closet and patch it up and fly it. Or you might salvage its motor for use in a U-control airplane you build yourself. The U-control airplane is a puppet, but you can have a good time with it and learn a few things about airspeed and the use of elevators as you continue on your way toward piloting a full-house, stand-off scale-model R/C airplane.

Another way you might put a small model engine to use is by getting into free-flight modeling. This teaches the student pilot about airfoil surfaces while he or she is out having some fun.

A free-flight model airplane has a long, spindly fuselage and even longer, gull-shaped wings. The wings are usually made in one piece, so that the free-flight airplane, like many R/C planes, actually has one solid wing. As in the R/C planes, the wing on a free-flight plane is held in place with heavy rubber bands. Large wings are somewhat hard to build. It takes a lot of parts and a lot of sanding to make one, and, in the process of covering it with tightly stretched fabric, wash-out or wash-in has to be avoided. Wash-out and wash-in are terms to describe the warpage in a poorly made wing. Wash-out and wash-in are not difficult to avoid or to correct, but once the wing is all properly made and covered, the modelist does not want that wing destroyed in a minor crash.

Thus the wing is attached with rubber bands which are strong enough to hold it in place during flight, but which will stretch and allow the wing to fall off in one piece when the airplane makes a hard landing. Free-flight airplanes often make hard landings, since they fly with no direction at all from the ground, and they sometimes fly for great distances. The free-flight model airplane is the potential runaway.

In the front it has an engine that looks too small for a plane of its size. But the free-flight airplane is extremely light, and its wings have the fat airfoil shape that gives the airplane the greatest possible lift characteristics. Racing airplanes have wings that are short and almost flat. Free-flight airplanes and gliders have long wings with a high, smooth upward bulge to them. The free-flight model airplane is really a powered glider, with an engine just large enough to get the plane up pretty high before it runs out of gas. Its rudder is fixed in one position, angled so that the plane will fly in circles. The rudder is very slightly angled, so that the circles will be wide ones and the plane won't lose altitude by making a sharp turn.

The object of the free-flighters' game is to see who can keep an airplane aloft for the longest time. The secret lies in the light weight of the plane and in the shape of the airfoil wing surfaces which give the plane its lift. The motor is almost incidental to winning a free-flight contest, because all the contestants use motors of the same size, and each has a timer that cuts off its fuel supply after a specified period of time.

People brought their planes from six different countries to compete in the National Free-Flight Society's recent meet in Taft, California. Taft is a great place for this sort of a contest, with little or no breeze to carry the silent and slowly circling planes too far out in the desert on their flights. These flights may last up to two hours after a two-minute period of climbing under engine power. An element of luck enters into free-flight contests, for a more poorly built airplane might wander into an updraft that will carry it far above all the other planes and win the blue ribbon for its builder. This same updraft may carry the plane so high that it runs into high altitude winds that carry it miles away from the contest. Some who attended the contest at Taft brought their trail bikes as well as their airplanes, so that they could chase their runaway powered gliders through the brush.

Free-flight, U-control, Peanut Scale planes are steps to take along the way to R/C flying. Whatever route you choose in getting into R/C flying, develop and practice your skills as you go, having a good time on your workbench and in the air.

7

Controlled Flight

As you read magazines and catalogs on R/C flying, you will probably see advertisements about pulse proportional radio gear. The ads say this is ideal for the beginning R/C modelist. It sounds good, and the radio gear as well as the specially designed planes for use with it seem inexpensive. But it is a primitive sort of R/C flying, and its cost by now is no less than that of more satisfying R/C flying.

Pulse proportional flying is one-channel flying. The gear is much smaller, but it does not provide for much more control than the R/C pioneers had on their planes of the 1930s. The planes for use with pulse systems are essentially powered gliders, but they don't have the excellent airfoil surfaces of either a free-flight plane or a respectable glider. A magnet with constantly reversing polarity is inside the airplane, attached to its rudder. The airplane's rudder flaps back and forth, until a command from the radio on the ground directs it to flap more on one side than the other, making the airplane turn and lose altitude.

It sounds more cumbersome than it really is. One of the two advantages of pulse proportional gear is its very small size. The modelist who wants to fly a really small R/C airplane might turn to this kind of gear, but miniaturized digital proportional gear has just about eliminated this advantage. The other advantage of pulse proportional gear has been its low cost, but mass production methods for digital gear have minimized this. If you can pick up used pulse proportional radio gear for ten or twenty dollars, you'll have some fun and learn things, but this system is falling by the wayside.

Cost is a deterrent to many who want to get into R/C flying. When I asked Felipe Sanders if he'd like to try R/C flying in addition to U-control racing, he said, "Sure! But it costs a thousand dollars to get into it."

He was quite surprised to hear that two-channel radios can be had for less than a hundred dollars. He would need at least a three-channel radio in order to use his .30 and .40 U-control engines with an R/C plane. But he could get off to the best kind of start in R/C flying by using a little .049 engine with an inexpensive two-channel radio and a glider.

R/C gliding is popular around San Diego because of the Torrey Pine Cliffs. A brisk ocean breeze blows against the four-hundred-foot cliffs constantly, providing a strong updraft for full-sized sailplanes and hang gliders and for R/C gliders. The breeze will keep either a soaring glider or a sturdy little aerobatic glider up in the air for hours. Club members of the Torrey Pines Gulls claim they can fly bricks off the cliffs, and they usually find time to help a novice launch and land his or her new R/C glider there. One mistake, however, sends the glider to the bottom of the cliffs. And such cliffs, with their reliably constant updrafts, are not to be found in every part of the country.

The gliding done at Torrey Pines is known as slope soaring. The steady breeze blowing against the cliffs does not simply blow up and over the top of the cliffs; it builds up against the face of the cliffs, forming a mass of constantly rising air that extends out to sea for several hundred yards. This provides excellent lift for the gliders at Torrey Pines. The same is true for gliders flown in other areas with similar conditions.

A few miles away from the cliffs is Mira Mesa, a very flat plain that is usually swept by a gentle breeze. It is typical of terrain to be found in many parts of the country. Many local R/C glider enthusiasts never go to the Torrey Pine Cliffs to fly, preferring instead to engage in thermal soaring at Mira Mesa.

A thermal soaring glider is built along the same lines as a free-flight plane, except that it has a larger fuselage to house the two-or three-channel radio gear, plus a little hook under the nose of the plane. The average breeze at Mira Mesa is not strong enough to take a glider like this aloft, and so the thermal soaring enthusiasts chipped in to get their own launcher.

The launcher consists of a large box with a car battery and a car starter inside it. The starter turns a reel on the outside of the box. A string on the reel runs a couple of hundred yards over cleared ground to a pulley, and from the pulley it runs back to a hook and a little red parachute by the box. A foot switch starts and stops the reel on the box. The hook on the string fits the hook under the nose of the glider. By tickling the foot switch and working the R/C rudder and elevators, the glider pilot can take his craft up several hundred feet, until it's directly over the pulley. The two hooks then disengage, and the parachute shows where the string is coming down. The thermal soaring glider is then on its own.

Thermal soaring involves seeking natural updrafts and riding them higher. Eagles and hawks do this. These natural updrafts are usually currents of warmer air, leisurely and invisibly spiraling upward from a sun-warmed spot on the ground. They're constantly changing position as they rise. The R/C pilot searches for them by guiding the airplane about and watching its wings. When a wing tip tilts up, the pilot turns the plane in the direction of that wing, and the glider will then go higher until the pilot loses that updraft. Under ideal thermal conditions, one of these gliders can stay aloft for hours. And with R/C control, the pilot doesn't have to have a trail bike to retrieve the plane.

Ideal conditions are rare. Electric winches are even more rare. They are fine for a club, where everyone can chip in with the money and time to build one, but they aren't much good for the individual flier. A much cheaper way to launch a thermal soaring glider is with a Hi-Start, but it's a very chancy way for the beginner to get off the ground. Hi-Start is a fancy name for a very long rubber band. One end is fixed to a point on the ground and the other hooked to the glider. The pilot walks back with the glider until the rubber band is stretched tight, and then lets the glider go. It really goes. With the rubber band at full tension, the glider zips out of the pilot's hands at very high speed. It has slowed down by the time it's rising up over the other end of the rubber band, if it's gotten that far. The trouble occurs in those first few yards, when the glider is going at maximum speed and the pilot is trying to reach the controls and use them. A Hi-Start is fine for the experienced glider pilot, especially if there's a friend along to help with the launching.

Thermal soaring gliders, stately birds with immense wing-spans of up to eight feet. This one has striped spoilers on its wings, operated by a third R/C channel.

Another type of R/C glider launching method calls for more than a friend. An R/C power plane fitted with a towline can take the glider aloft. The towline hook and the hook on the glider can be disengaged by maneuvering the two planes. Or the hook on the glider can be disengaged through radio control. This launching method, like all those mentioned so far, involves special equipment or special conditions that aren't always at hand. But there is a safe and easy way for the glider pilot to get in the air without any special conditions or launching equipment. The man who offers a very good package for this is the man who created Jonathan Livingston Seagull.

Jonathan Livingston Seagull is the philosophical bird who came to life in a book written by Richard Bach and in a movie made by Paramount Pictures. Paramount contacted a young man named Mark Smith to design and build a life-sized seagull, made out of fiberglass and fully controllable by R/C gear. Mark did an excellent job of it. His seagull-shaped glider flew very well and fooled the movie-goers. The reason that Mark and his father, Rod, were contacted to make the fiberglass hulls was because of their excellent reputation in designing the R/C gliders they distribute through Mark's Models, Inc.

Mark's latest glider is called the *Wanderer*. It has a six-foot wingspan, it satisfies the needs of both the thermal soaring pilots and the Torrey Pines fans, and it flies so easily that the novice can handle it once it's up in the air. And Mark and his father have designed into the

Wanderer the means of getting it up there without any updrafts or winches or tow planes or rubber bands.

The *Wanderer* was designed to have the option of a .049 engine in its nose. The engine does not come with the kit. In the kit, however, is a little plastic 33 1/3 record that gives the novice kit builder some tips on construction and even more valuable tips on how to trim the airplane and get it up in the air under engine power.

Mark Smith, designer and builder of Jonathon Livingston Seagull, and the designer of the Wanderer, an excellent R/C airplane to start into R/C sporting.

It's a fine glider. Experienced glider pilots build it without the motor and use the other methods to get it up in the air. After the novice has learned how to fly using cheap and reliable engine power to take the airplane aloft, the engine and prop can be removed and replaced with a smoothly aerodynamic nose block. By starting off under the power of a small engine, however, the panicky takeoff is eliminated, and the novice can concentrate on learning how to fly.

The plans for Mark Smith's *Wanderer* carry a small but important warning. It should be heeded by everyone involved in R/C sports—"A Radio-Controlled Model is not a 'toy'. Care and caution must be taken in properly building the model as well as in the installation and use of the Radio Control device. It is important to follow all the directions as to construction of this kit as well as installation and use of the engine and radio gear. The advice and assistance of a well-experienced builder and pilot is highly recommended. Don't take chances. Improper building or flying of this model could result in serious bodily injury to others, yourself or property damage."

Any airplane, including a glider, has to go through a preparation and checkout before it can fly safely.

Four large, new rubber bands should be used to secure the glider's wing to the fuselage. There is a balance point for the plane which is shown on the plans. The wing, as well as the radio gear, must be in place to check the balance point and trim the plane so it has the right balance. The balance point is checked at the root of the wing. The balance is trimmed by using lead fishing weights inside the nose or inside the tail. Excessive weight is certainly a consideration in flying, but most gliders with decent wingspans will lift several ounces of lead in addition to their radio gear. When you're flying regularly, you may want to add quite a few lead sinkers at the balance point of your glider, to give it more penetration on gusty, windy days. But when you start this sport use as little ballast as possible for trimming the plane, since you should test fly it on a calm day with a wind of less than 5 mph.

Your radio gear should already be in the plane. The plans for any glider should show how and where to mount it. If they do not, the radio gear should be mounted with the balance point in mind, and it must be mounted firmly and securely. Many flying modelists, anticipating some hard landings, wrap their receivers in foam rubber. A servo tray is best for mounting the servos. However they're mounted, they must be placed firmly so that the control surfaces and not the servos move on command.

The plans also will have illustrated how to install the control rods between the servos and the control surfaces. Stiff metal rods are favored, and nylon rods running inside a nylon sheath make a good second choice. The rods should have little if any lateral play in them, and braces may be needed to keep them stiff and still allow them to move as they should. Control rods and radio gear varies, and even the best plans can't cover all methods of installation.

The rods are attached to brackets, called control horns, on the glider's rudder and elevators. These brackets, and often the servos, are attached to the control rods with a hinge called a clevis. The clevis has a screw adjustment on it that permits the rudder to be adjusted vertically and the elevators horizontally when the servos are in the neutral position.

The batteries should be charged overnight before you go out on your test flight, and all the radio gear should be checked out before you leave your workbench. With the switch on the airplane and on the transmitter in the on position, check to see that the rudder and elevators function properly. Pulling back on the control stick should make the elevators go up, not down. When the plane is all checked out and balanced, turn off the two switches and take your plane and your gear to a nice big field of tall grass.

Face into the wind when you launch your airplane. Airplanes always take off and land into the wind. Launch it firmly and evenly, aiming for a spot on the ground some fifty or seventy-five feet in front of you. If you try to give it some altitude by launching it upward, it can stall and send you right back to the workbench. As it glides, you can tell if it is nose-heavy or tail-heavy, and you can add some more weights as necessary. Make several test glides without the controls and without the engine running if you have built a powered glider of the *Wanderer* type. Keep making the test flights until your glider is running straight and true.

With your equipment all checked out, with your FCC

license in your pocket, you should be ready to take off in a controlled flight.

Fill up the tank on your engine and get it going. Switches on, and with an airplane in one hand and a transmitter in the other, make a final check on the workings of the control surfaces. Then launch the glider just as you did when you were checking it out for trim.

It will climb up and away from you, and you will experience the feeling of breathless elation that is so much a part of R/C flying. Enjoy it, but don't stand there watching as your airplane climbs up out of radio range and out of sight.

Keep your wits about you. Do not overcontrol your glider as you make a slow turn to bring the airplane around. There is safety in height, so try for some altitude, but don't try to angle it upward so quickly that it loses airspeed and stalls. You should already be thinking about making a landing on this, your first flight. And you should be mentally placing yourself in your cockpit, with that left-right confusion in mind.

Straighten it out. Try a little sharper turn and see how much altitude the airplane will lose. Keep slowly circling, trying for an altitude of two hundred or three hundred feet while you still have the engine pulling you up in the air. Don't think about doing any stunts yet. Just learn how to turn your airplane while still maintaining altitude. Keep thinking about landing into the wind in the same direction the plane was launched.

When the engine runs out of fuel, straighten out the airplane. Take your hands off the controls and see how well the airplane glides by itself. You may wish to trim the controls a bit now with the tabs on the transmitter. Keep the airplane circling, keep the wings as level as you can, and make an imaginary approach to an invisible landing field a hundred feet over your head. Keep up your airspeed.

You may have some trouble bringing it down. On a breezy day a good glider will want to stay up in the air. Circle the field again, easing the stick forward to bring it down on a long, shallow approach. Later on you can spin and loop to lose altitude for your approach, but not at first. Keep the airspeed up, don't let it float as it heads for its landing. Just before it touches down, ease back on the stick to make the plane flare into the start of a stall as it settles gently down on its skid.

Don't feel badly if you have to walk to the spot where your glider landed. Pilots of full-sized planes say that a good landing is a landing the pilot can walk away from. A good landing for an R/C pilot is the landing the pilot can walk to and find the radio gear still intact.

The radio gear is sturdier than the airplane. You will have some rough landings and some airframe damage while sharpening your skills on training flights. Essential is some five-minute epoxy cement to make field repairs. With or without the very considerable help you can get from an experienced pilot, you should have several hours of simple, straightforward controlled flight under your belt before you go on to stunting and R/C power flying.

8

R/C Flying

Before you do any serious R/C flying, join the AMA. This is not the American Medical Association, but the Academy of Model Aeronautics. It offers inexpensive insurance that covers a flying mishap that may damage someone else's property. Its address is 815 15th Street, N.W., Washington, D.C. 20005.

With insurance coverage, you can do some stunting more comfortably with your two-channel glider, and you can go on from this to the more complex aerobatic maneuvers possible with multichannel equipment. The other "insurance" you should have before you try any stunting is the insurance of altitude. The rule is to have enough altitude to allow for two consecutive mistakes in the air before trying any stunts.

A loop is very simple. Dive to gain speed, haul back on the stick for full up elevator until the plane goes up and over, and at the bottom of the loop, ease the stick forward and level off.

If your airspeed isn't up to allowing you to complete the loop, give the plane full rudder to roll it over and make it fall into level flight before it stalls. If you're into a good, fast loop and give your airplane full rudder just before it goes into the top of the loop, and then immediately neutralize the controls for level flight, the plane will be flying right side up again. And it will be headed back in the direction from which it came. This is the Immelmann loop, made famous by one of the Red Baron's flying buddies in World War I.

To do a wingover, gain some airspeed by diving, level off, and send the plane up by hauling back on the stick. Then push the stick back to neutral and simultaneously give the plane some rudder, and the plane will go from the start of a climb into a wingover turn.

Slow rolls are similarly done, and they are a joy to behold. Get up some speed, start to climb, and give the plane full rudder. As it inverts, push forward on the stick to keep it from losing altitude while it's upside down. As it completes the roll, ease off on the controls.

Really violent stunting can't be done with a long-winged glider. Trying to get too much out of this type of plane can stretch the rubber bands to a point where the wing and fuselage make separate landings.

You may wish to continue with two-channel flying by getting a short-winged power plane. There are small power plane kits that call for a .049 engine, fitted with a larger gas tank, and which have ailerons in place of a rudder for making turns. Ailerons are the long, hinged control surfaces on the trailing edges of the wings. One swings up while the other swings down, banking the airplane into a turn. Ailerons are needed for full aerobatic capability, but this capability can't be there at the sacrifice of the rudder control.

There are also small model power planes with only rudder and elevator control, but these don't provide much more aerobatic opportunity than the two-channel glider. None of these two-channel power planes has a throttle control, and you will feel limited by operating an airplane at full power all the time. Your two-channel radio can get you into quite a few different airplanes, but sooner or later you'll want to trade it in for a multichannel set.

A four-channel radio is recommended for R/C flying, even though only three of its channels may be used at first. The third channel may be used to operate ailerons on an aerobatic glider, but these gliders need strong updrafts, like those at the Torrey Pine Cliffs, to be put through their paces. The third channel would be used for ailerons on a power plane, too, with the fourth being used for throttle control. With four channels of operation, the power plane now has all the necessary functions of a full-sized airplane. This is the full-house model plane.

Start with a training airplane. Power planes do not fly as easily as gliders, and advanced power planes do not fly well at all in the hands of a novice power plane pilot. Sig Manufacturing Company, among many others, makes kits for training planes that are easy to build, easy to fly, and good for some basic stunting. The training plane will have to be large enough to contain your four-channel radio gear, and therefore it will have to have an engine that's larger than the .049 you may have used on that power-assisted glider. Your new engine should be broken in at the workbench before you go power flying, and you should have an experienced R/C power plane pilot with you to help you learn how to fly this quick, responsive plane.

Learn how to taxi the airplane before you try to take it off the ground. This will give you some feel for the throttle and rudder controls. You will not be able to make any test glides with your new power plane, since most of these planes are definitely not good at gliding. Your first flights should be made with the engine idle set as low as possible. It should be set so low that the prop doesn't pull the idling airplane forward through closely clipped grass. Some pilots use a drag brake on the wheels to keep the idling airplane from creeping along over the asphalt. The importance of having the engine set at low idle speed on your first flights, however, is in the landing, not the taxiing.

A low idle speed permits a slow, safe landing. By this time in your career as an R/C pilot you'll be able to bring an airplane in on its approach pattern without stalling it. But if the engine is idling too fast, your first landings may come on too quickly for you to handle. You can wait till the fast-idling plane runs out of gas before you try to land it, but then you will only have that one chance to bring it down safely, for it will not circle the field for another approach when it's out of gas.

Take off and land your new airplane repeatedly. Practice touch-and-go landings. Get used to the throttle and the ailerons. You'll be using your ailerons more than your rudder now to keep your new airplane in level flight. Just as you did with your glider, work your way into stunting gradually. Practice the airplane's ground handling, remembering that even if it has a nose wheel it is the rudder that steers it when it's on the ground. And when you're ready to take it up and stunt with it, allow yourself all the altitude you would need to recover from two flying mistakes made in a row.

You will probably base the selection of your training plane on practicality rather than looks. Your trainer is a plane that might well be destroyed by a beginner's mistake. Some airplanes, advertised as training planes, are so aerobatically designed that they will not recover from a spin, so be careful of your selection. Listen to the advice of the hobby shop proprietor, but be aware that the proprietor does not handle all manufacturers' lines. The advice you get from other power plane hobbyists and that which you find in magazines like *Model Builder* is usually most acceptable.

Your trainer will be an airplane you'll always be fond of, but you'll probably graduate into something fancier. Your further entry into R/C flying will now be strictly up to you. There are quite a few ways for you to go. With your student days behind you, you can go on and build and fly the airplane that has the most personal appeal to you.

You may want to build a pattern plane. These are fast airplanes designed to fly the stunt patterns that AMA officials have set up for stunt competition. In competition, every contestant flies the same set of maneuvers, and pattern planes are especially designed to do well in these nationally held contests. If you're good at stunting with your trainer, you'll do well with a pattern plane as you learn the series of precision maneuvers carried out by the expert pilots at AMA-sponsored meets.

If you like speed, you might look into getting a pylon racer. Pylon racers have special racing engines, and their airframes are designed to conform to AMA pylon racing rules. Formula I pylon racers use .40 engines to reach speeds of 140 mph, while the smaller and considerably less expensive ¼ Midget class pylon racers fly with .15 engines. AMA-sponsored pylon races are not held very often, but flying clubs frequently stage informal club pylon races to satisfy their members' needs for speed.

Meticulous craftsmen are attracted to scale-model airplanes. Stand-off scale airplanes are those planes that are judged for realism by experts who stand off a few yards and try to detect any deviations from the reality of the model airplane's full-sized prototype. Some stand-off scale modelists use little trails of epoxy cement to simulate a weld that was on a prototype plane. Others have been known to position individually 20,000 simulated rivet heads to reproduce the total picture of a World War II warplane.

Scale-model planes should have all the original airplane's functions, such as a retractable landing gear, a sliding cockpit canopy, and a four-bladed prop. These airplanes also have to perform in the air at speeds that are realistically to scale. It takes some sort of carefree courage to send hundreds of dollars and thousands of hours of work into the air in hope of winning a trophy, but the stand-off scale model is a favorite with R/C pilots.

Biplanes are great fun to build and fly, not only for the nostalgia buff, but for the stunting enthusiast and the scale modelist as well. Biplanes are very responsive and quite tricky to handle. Biplanes and triplanes and antique monoplanes challenge flying ability as well as craftsmanship, and invariably attract a good deal of attention at any miniature aerodrome.

Multiengine airplane models present even greater challenges than do biplanes. Their construction can take months or even years, and it takes an exceedingly cool hand to bring all that work safely to the ground if one engine dies in the air. But seeing an old Ford trimotor monoplane flying over the field might start you off on building a miniature version of the late Howard Hughes's six-engined *Spruce Goose*.

Sport planes are by far the largest category of R/C power planes. These can compete in a great many different kinds of events, but they're mainly just for sporting around with a model airplane. They come in all sizes and don't have to look like anything else that's ever been in the air before. They just have to be fun to fly.

There are other model airplanes for those who have a severe case of modeler's disease. You can buy a little jet engine that will move your model MIG-21 through the air at startling speeds, testing your flying skills and coordination to the limit. On the opposite end of the Peanut Scale, some manufacturers specialize in kits for R/C planes with giant ten-foot wingspans. You can get a kit for a fully functional helicopter, which, when completed, will send you back to flight training school, since these rather expensive aircraft don't fly at all like a fixed-wing aircraft. You can get miniature skis for your trainer so you can land and take off from the snow, and these little accessories represent only a very tiny part of the dazzling array of miniature accessories that may be a part of the airplanes you build and fly.

Or you can get an all-electric plane. Only a few manufacturers are offering electric planes at this time, but as smaller servos and more powerful batteries are developed this form of R/C flying continues to grow. Astro-Flight is one manufacturer that handles all you'll need in order to try out a form of R/C flying that does away with fuel, engine-starting problems, and engine noise.

The electric model airframe is built very light, since power-to-weight ratios in electric planes are not as great as they are with gas engine planes. Electric airplanes are slower than gas engine planes, and this makes the electric plane especially suitable for crafting one of those old-time airplanes that had to struggle down the runway to get up in the air. Electric airplanes also eliminate the worst of the problems of the multiengined fuel-powered model airplane, since electric motors start up at the flick of a switch and can be easily synchronized to take such a model through aerobatic maneuvers.

Bob Boucher is the owner of Astro-Flight and one of the primary developers of the electric airplane. It's a pleasure to see his Victor P-68 on a runway. A puff of white smoke bursts out from under each wing as Bob presses the button that sends life to its twin engines. The airplane taxis smoothly to a starting line and pauses there to wait for flight instructions. Off it goes, gradually climbing over the tarmac, then banking around the field as it gains altitude. Its motors make no noise at all, but the sound from its props is scale-model perfect as it cuts through the air, rolling and looping over the upturned faces of the crowd. The P-68 makes a nice, smooth landing and taxis up to the feet of the giant with the control box in his hands. Its spinning props come to rest, and its servos wait for their next command.

Bob puts on a remarkable demonstration with his electric airplanes. But upstairs at his place of business is an airplane more remarkable than any of those he sells. It is quite a large model airplane. The top of its wing is completely covered with silicon wafers, for this radio-controlled model airplane's propeller gets all its power from the sun beating down on its solar cells. And it flies.

9

The Expanding World of R/C

You know you can't get all the way into every form of R/C modeling and sporting. There just isn't time. But you can try.

Wesley Jung is trying, and doing pretty well. At eighteen, he doesn't have the time or the money to compete in stand-off scale flying events, to build and sail a working model of the *Titanic*, or to compete in the World Cup R/C Car Race each year. But, with a two-channel radio and limited funds, Wesley is actively into land, water, and air R/C sports.

His land machine is an electrically driven, fiberglass-bodied dune buggy. He zips it around in his backyard, on the school grounds, out in the back country, over any kind of miniature rough terrain he chooses.

His boat uses the same servos and motor, but with different gearing. He made his boat out of Styrofoam surfboard scrap and fitted it out with a cabin he made from scrap wood. Wes's boat isn't as pretty as the tugboats and schooners on the model yacht ponds, but it zips in and out among them with its own brand of homemade charm.

His airplane is a glider kit, a *Spirit of '76*, made completely out of preformed Styrofoam and ready to fly when its parts have been snapped together and his radio gear has been transferred from his boat or car to the plane. Wes's glider doesn't handle as well as a *Wanderer*, but it certainly flies well enough to satisfy his vicarious longings to be in the sky with the birds.

Like all R/Cers, Wes is limited by the money he has to spend, the skills he has at his command, and the patience he uses in putting those skills to work. Wes's limitations are changing. He's earning a little more money now, and he's using some of that along with what he's learned about boats to build a racing boat. He wants an electric power plane, but he can't afford the four-channel radio gear it would take for a full-house model airplane. He's patient enough to save up his money for that while he enjoys what he has. Wes has plenty of time, and he might well wind up getting all the way into every form of R/C modeling and sporting.

Wolfgang Matt and Hanno Pretner are all the way into R/C stunt flying. These two young men are European R/C stunt flying champions, and they frequently appear on TV in Europe, giving quick demonstrations of their skills as part of their lucrative endorsements of commercial products quite unrelated to R/C modeling.

Most of the air force pilots of both Israel and Pakistan are R/C pilots as well, since building and flying an R/C model is part of their formal military training. It teaches them basic airframe construction and flying techniques, and as they are making repairs in the aftermath of a crash, it gives them time to think about the human repairs that might be necessary if their careless handling crashed a full-sized airplane.

The enjoyments of R/C can come from many diverse corners of its small world. Larry Young, the man who is building the R/C gear for Cy Steele's B-25, has no desire to pilot a model airplane. But he's looking forward to the time when he can smile up at the sky as the product of his electronic workbench goes streaking past, opening bomb bay doors as it crosses the field. There is no end to innovations in the world of R/C, the most recent being sidecar motorcycle racing now being enjoyed in England. Japanese travelers, enthralled with the notion of American dune buggies, took that idea back to their own overcrowded country and brought it to life in the small world of R/C. R/C sporting crosses every boundary line, and its language is understood all over the world.

In that world of R/C you may learn about all sorts of things like clevises and the wing-loading factor in airplanes, and about battery chargers, mizzen masts, centrifugal clutches, and thermodynamics. But the basic reason for its growing popularity is recreation. Have a good time!

Index